BELIEFS
AND
SOCIAL
INTELLIGENCE

C. Margaret Hall

Beliefs and Social Intelligence *is a guide to discovering the power and complexity of beliefs and social influences, as well as the impacts they have on our freedom and opportunities. This book is dedicated to readers who want to better themselves, their accomplishments, and the world we live in.*

Table of Contents

Social Sources of Beliefs

Social Intelligence and Beliefs

What Kind of World?

Social Sources of Beliefs

I. Families

Our families are primary sources of many of our beliefs, particularly of the most deep-seated and influential beliefs in our behavior and actions. Our beliefs are crucial aspects of our being and doing, largely because they develop from our closest relationships, as well as from our most compelling emotional experiences. Our families help us to develop the passions and emotions that move us to act most forcefully. Consequently, when we examine how we acquire our beliefs, and what they mean to us, we become aware of how much our families influence us in the critical processes of defining ourselves, others, and our worlds.

We often think that our beliefs derive from our education, or from broad political influences. However, our predispositions to accept particular educational or political beliefs are largely acquired through our interactions with our families. For example, we are attracted to specific educational or political beliefs because of emphases given by our parents, siblings, or emotionally significant others. This means that when we decide we want to change our beliefs, we must first understand the family origins of our beliefs, in order to be effective in making these changes. Even though other major social influences also affect our beliefs and belief systems, we especially need to change how we act and react in our family exchanges, in order to modify our beliefs in ways that will truly make a difference in the long run.

1

Beliefs and Social Intelligence

When we are young, our families make decisions for us, which in large part determine how we approach our families, religions, social classes, cultures, and societies. As we grow older, we begin to see ourselves and others in the contexts of our families, religions, social classes, cultures, and societies, so that we gradually become actors in these increasingly impersonal social circles. Ultimately, when we know how to use the broad perspectives of social intelligence, we necessarily realize that we are historical actors. This includes using our chosen beliefs in all our everyday interactions with others, so that we can have constructive impacts on our different social worlds.

Social intelligence helps us to cultivate our awareness of ourselves as historical actors. For example, our beliefs increase their meaning, purpose, and direction when we work toward increasing our social intelligence. This enables us to act more decisively in directions which increase social justice, because social intelligence limits how others direct or curtail what we do, which would otherwise diminish the meaningfulness of our everyday choices. Furthermore, social intelligence shows us that when we understand the power and complexity of our families and social influences, we manage our beliefs and options more effectively.

Continuing to be realistically critical of how we acquired our beliefs about our families, religions, social classes, cultures, and societies increases our freedom. Families, religions, social classes, cultures, and societies are ever-broadening social spheres of significant social activities, which influence many of our motivations and energies. Becoming more objective about how these social influences affect our behavior, enables us to decide whether we want to continue or replace those beliefs which we have already acquired in our families, religions, social classes, cultures, and societies.

Some ethical principles are based on the fact that we become more responsible when we clarify the orientations of our actions. Such increased clarity lets us construct more effective strategies to change our beliefs where necessary, and to act more deliberately toward achieving social justice. We can improve the quality of our worlds—our beliefs are meaningful starting points for many different kinds of individual and social changes—because beliefs strongly influence our ideas, ideals, and values.

We accomplish these tasks more effectively when we examine clusters of our beliefs as well as our relatively isolated beliefs. We find, for example, that being Christian or Jewish gives us specific ways to define ourselves and social realities. Related values in individual religions are foundations for beliefs that provide us with ready-made explanations of ourselves and the world.

Although plugging into traditional belief systems may comfort us, and possibly increase the meaning of our everyday routines, they do not consistently serve us well in crisis situations. Social intelligence helps us to assess the validity of clusters of our beliefs, so that we become more knowledgeable about how to construct and select beliefs that are both dependable and predictable in their effects.

When we use social intelligence to understand specific relationships among our beliefs, we need to look closely at the basic beliefs in our own families and other families. Identifying patterns in our families' basic beliefs helps us to recognize their power in our lives. This also helps us to appreciate the uniqueness of our families' beliefs more fully, as well as to respect the uniqueness of other families' beliefs. Social intelligence guides us in identifying, supporting, and reinforcing differences among families' beliefs as important priorities.

One of the more destructive aspects of families' beliefs is their tendencies to closure because of their repetitions. Dogmatic beliefs, for example, are rigidified through habitual applications in families, which make them very difficult to change, even though dogmatic beliefs have negative

3

consequences for most family members. However, when we discover rigidity in our own family beliefs, we can use social intelligence to replace such problematic dogmatism, by cultivating more open and more flexible family beliefs.

Using social intelligence to change family beliefs, in order to increase openness in our families and others' families, brings many benefits. For example, the increased openness in our families ultimately helps us to nurture social justice, because our overall priorities are re-established, and we can more easily and more effectively contribute to developing an inclusive common good.

Basic Family Beliefs

The most basic beliefs we hold about our families, and our families' views of ourselves, others, and the world, focus on the nature of human nature and the functions that families fulfill. Because families are found in all societies, and are documented to have existed before community settlements were widespread, we must acknowledge families' capacities to endure and help us to survive. Protection, nourishment, personal care, and support are some of the fundamental ways in which families meet individual, family, and societal needs to perpetuate themselves.

Our beliefs about our basic needs and basic natures influence how we define, describe, and explain our existence and our potentials. These parameters underlie all the beliefs we refine and apply to different aspects of our existence. Our beliefs about religions, social classes, cultures, and societies, for example, are built on our beliefs about our families, and about our basic human nature. Therefore, in order to make effective changes in these other social spheres, we must first examine and modify our beliefs about our families.

One of the basic family beliefs many of us have in our modern, present-day societies, is that optimally love should exist among family members. However, social intelligence suggests that it is only when our families' love includes some social and emotional distance, as well as objectivity, that our involvement with relatives can be truly productive and positive. If love suffocates our individuality, for example, so that beliefs in family togetherness override beliefs based on family and social realities, family relationships and individuals' goals are jeopardized. Therefore, this basic family belief about love among family members needs to be critiqued and tempered, to some extent, so that we are aware of how oppression and exploitation can infiltrate family relationships and family togetherness in the guise of love.

Contemporary family beliefs in the importance of parenting may also produce negative consequences. For example, when we put the comfort of our children above all else, we may reduce our children's capacities to fend for themselves. To the extent that we overprotect members of the younger generations of our families, we pollute what should be important family and social priorities, so that the well-being of all may be threatened.

Another basic family belief, which should be questioned, is our long-established priority that our families should be made secure by amassing material goods. Although there is no doubt that protection and material needs are important, they are not all-important, and they do not necessarily create optimal living conditions for all family members. Rather, we should question the extent to which we believe that security and material goods contribute to our families' welfare, because ultimately we need more intangible goods and services in order to survive and do well. Inspiration and companionship, for example, may often be more significant or more grounded social influences which define our individual and family well-being.

Similarly, it is not so much our belief in the importance of parenting our children, in its own right, that is critical for individual and social fulfillment, as how our children are socialized by our families, and how our families define themselves, others, and the world. The content of our basic family beliefs must include particular human values if we are to raise strong children, and make the world a better place. For example, we are more effective parents when we encourage our children to cherish their own life-enhancing values and beliefs, rather than when we try to create social beings in our own images.

In considering later stages of the life cycle, our basic family beliefs suggest that we have some responsibility to care for elderly and infirm members of our families until they die. Although family elders may not need orientations to the world in the same ways that members of younger generations do, we should define elders' needs for care in socially intelligent, humane ways. For example, being effectively oriented to death may be as important a need as being oriented to life. Consequently, we need to enter into deliberately chosen exchanges with our elders, perhaps about their illnesses or deaths, in order to create optimal conditions for later stages in their lives as well as ours.

Ideally, our most basic beliefs about our families should be open to making improvements. We start to understand which of our basic beliefs about our families need to be changed, and how we can accomplish these changes, by examining our traditional ways of thinking and believing about our families. Next, we choose to modify some of these beliefs to increase openness in our families, perhaps so that the experiences of our youngest and oldest family members will be enhanced. In this way our basic family beliefs are no longer fixed or unmovable. Furthermore, when we increase the fluidity and flexibility of our families' basic beliefs, we improve the quality of life for all our family members.

Unique Family Beliefs

Our families' beliefs express distinctiveness and differences from other families, as well as similarities in shared basic needs. Furthermore, our families have so many varied beliefs, that we often focus more on the uniqueness of our families' beliefs than on their shared characteristics, in order to personalize our understanding of our families. However, when we use social intelligence to examine our families' beliefs, we pay attention to both the differences and the similarities of beliefs within our families and among families.

Unique family beliefs derive from the wide range of differences that are found within our families. Although we generalize about our families' beliefs in important ways—such as identifying the most important values which our families have—the distinctiveness of the patterns of interactions in our families creates unique beliefs in our families about possibilities and options. Because of the overall richness of our families' basic and unique beliefs, our families guide us in socializing our children, caring for elderly relatives, and meeting family needs for protection or material goods.

When considering the significance of our unique family beliefs, we need to examine not only differences in our families' interpretations of their basic family needs, but also differences in their wide ranges of interactions. For example, our unique family beliefs are produced by our families' emotional dependencies—such as between parents and children—and particular patterns of emotional dependencies exist in all families. Social intelligence helps us to appreciate significant nuances in our own families' emotional dependencies, which influence our unique family beliefs, both within and among families.

Family uniqueness must be cherished through our families' beliefs because our distinctiveness gives us our most important and most meaningful identities. For example, if we consider only ways in which we are like others, we may not see possibilities that our unique talents and creativity could achieve. Also, when we see contrasts in families' relationships and actions, new opportunities and choices emerge, so that we discover viable new ways to deal with recurring family problems. Therefore, it is essential to honor family uniqueness, which is partly maintained by our unique family beliefs, because it yields different ways to think and act that are beyond the reach of our already-established customs and traditions.

An easy way to appreciate the significance of unique family beliefs is to assess the wide range of different beliefs about individuality in our own families. When we ask our relatives what their views and assumptions are about themselves within our own families, for example, we discover that no two family members see themselves and our families in the same way, and that the range of variability in relatives' beliefs about individual uniqueness within our own families is substantial. This pattern is amplified and compounded when we also consider unique family beliefs in others' families.

Social intelligence shows us that we need both to share similar, basic beliefs about our families, and to express an infinite range of unique possibilities for family interactions and family beliefs. Social intelligence requires us to focus on both our basic and unique family beliefs, in order to grasp the shared roots and awesome breadth of these differences. Doing this gives us the advantage of increasing the flexibility, rather than the rigidity, of our families' beliefs and assumptions.

Our beliefs also become more flexible when we ask ourselves how our families are affected by our religions, social classes, cultures, and societies. For example, to what extent are our family beliefs related to our religious, social class, cultural, and societal beliefs? Also, how do the emotional qualities of our family beliefs affect other social spheres of our daily lives?

Because some of these questions are answered in the next chapters in the Social Sources of Beliefs section of *Beliefs and Social Intelligence*, it is sufficient to note here that the complexity of relationships among different social systems— families, religions, social classes, cultures, and societies— reinforces our intrinsic interdependence. We are necessarily conditioned, by our families, to orient ourselves and our worlds with regard to these varied social spheres. Optimally, our family relationships respond to our interactions with our religions, social classes, cultures, and societies, so that these broad social influences help to strengthen and deepen our emotional roots in our families. As we do this, both our shared similarities in families' beliefs, and the unique characteristics of our families' beliefs, affect how we conduct ourselves with others in our daily tasks and our strategies to increase social intelligence and social justice.

We create more beliefs in possibilities for improved futures through these endeavors, when we respect both the similarities and uniqueness of our family beliefs. Wide ranges of family beliefs yield numerous possibilities for whatever we decide to do, including how we choose or design specific strategies and goals. Social intelligence helps us to realize that human potential is rich, as well as limited. Because of this fact, we should aim toward achieving flexibility, rather than rigidity, in our family beliefs, thereby increasing our social intelligence and social justice.

Rigid Family Beliefs

The fact that shared family beliefs tend to rigidify through time is problematic for family well-being. When this happens, families' capacities to adapt to changing circumstances are limited. In fact, sometimes family beliefs become so rigid that they create imbalances and dysfunctions in their family members' exchanges, especially among relatives in different generations.

An example of a rigid family belief, which has pernicious consequences for all family members, is family standards for selecting spouses. A family's beliefs about which spouses are socially acceptable to elders may become increasingly narrowed and bound by traditions. These rigid family standards essentially suffocate their family members. Even though their young adults may prefer to select prospective dates, partners, or spouses according to their elders' outdated personal or family criteria, their actual choices all too easily bring heartbreak, or even family schisms, around these issues of new dates, partnerships, or spouses.

Social intelligence helps us to be more aware of the harmful results of rigid family beliefs through examining all family beliefs. In deciding which family beliefs we want to influence our interactions with our relatives and others, we need to distinguish between beliefs that are flexible and functional, and beliefs that are rigid and dysfunctional. Social intelligence helps us to understand how flexible family beliefs allow our families to adapt to social pressures more effectively, as well as strengthen their capacities to be innovative. Having these criteria clearly in mind prevents what would otherwise be automatic tendencies of our families to cling to their rigid beliefs, which restrict rather than free their family members.

Because of the frequency of everyday family exchanges, which most importantly include interactions among several generations, and because of the emotional support that families give their members, beliefs are transmitted as a matter of course in families' daily activities. When families' neediness is increased during family crises such as the death of a child, family beliefs are magnified and rigidified in their relatives' urgent exchanges. Furthermore, because rigid family beliefs are difficult to change back to more flexible beliefs, they are internalized and concentrated through their family members' continued use.

Another factor which influences, or increases, the rigidity of family beliefs is the dominance of particular relatives in families. Family members are often manipulated when the dominant relatives' beliefs are both dogmatic and widely accepted within their families. Although dominant family members' beliefs may be tacitly internalized by their relatives, because they appear to represent their families' beliefs, these beliefs are likely to be used or abused by the dominant family members to maintain the family status quo in favor of the dominant family members' interests. The rigidity of their beliefs makes it easier for the dominant family members to compel other relatives to conform to their wishes, so that the non-dominant family members no longer act on their own behalf.

Rigid family beliefs often close family emotional systems. As a result, families perpetuate their outdated beliefs, which ultimately prevent these families' innovations and most successful adaptations. Family schisms are also more likely to develop and disrupt family connections when families' beliefs are rigid, unless some direct or deliberate action is taken to cultivate more flexible family beliefs.

First hand experiences of dominant relatives' rigid family beliefs are usually uncomfortable and distinctly unpleasant. We feel imposed upon, exploited, or oppressed in these circumstances, and we may react to such family control by breaking away from our families temporarily, or by withdrawing from our entire family emotional systems for long periods of time. These reactions are relatively frantic or desperate attempts to meet our deep-seated needs for freedom, often made with the hope that we can re-establish contacts with our families that are more to our liking at a later time. Our ideal, which social intelligence helps us to attain, is usually that new patterns of family interaction will develop, so that we can have more flexible family beliefs and family bonds in the future.

Overall, family dogmas and bigotries frequently plague our families and societies. Rigid family beliefs are like cancers, in that they often have strangle-holds on our families, which threaten our families' abilities to perpetuate themselves and enhance family members' lives. Rigid beliefs, dogmas, and bigotries reduce relatives' contributions to the common good and social justice, so that consequently both families and societies suffer.

Because social intelligence helps us to modify or discard our rigid family beliefs, social intelligence is one of our most constructive long term solutions to these problems. Social intelligence shows us how to cultivate more functional and more meaningful beliefs, so that we can substitute these for our dysfunctional, rigid family beliefs. For example, increasing our beliefs in the importance of autonomy and freedom for all family members ultimately makes our entire families stronger. These new, more effective bases of family commitments generate additional constructive beliefs, so that we gradually improve our families' actions, both within and outside our families.

Flexible Family Beliefs

In contrast to families with rigid beliefs, families with flexible beliefs expressly allow for many different family members' interpretations of how these families expect their members to behave. Families with flexible beliefs give their relatives more latitude and leeway to think independently, and to express varied viewpoints, than families with rigid beliefs. Although families with flexible beliefs may have some clusters of values or beliefs that are readily identifiable, these families move more closely in accordance with the changing times of societies, than families with rigid beliefs. Families with flexible beliefs also support family members who want to establish innovative lifestyles or creative new ventures.

Flexible family beliefs are more life-enhancing, as well as more supportive of all family members, than rigid family beliefs. There are relatively few restrictive sanctions in families with flexible beliefs, and their sanctions are usually not tied to pressures to conform to particular family beliefs. Because direct encouragement is given to family members who want to experiment with new activities in families with flexible beliefs, changes are expected in families with flexible beliefs, rather than reinforcements or repetitions of the status quo.

In these ways families with flexible beliefs characteristically give their members considerable breathing space to define their behaviors, so that they grow more easily into their own particular understandings of maturity. Furthermore, the dominance of a few family members, that often characterizes many families with rigid family beliefs, usually does not occur in families with flexible beliefs. This means that flexible family beliefs, rather than rigid family beliefs, engender conditions that promote freedom in family exchanges, as well as freedom for family members' participation in societies.

Flexible family beliefs are neither wishy-washy, nor without integrity. In fact, families with flexible beliefs often remain steadfast in their ways, valuing their flexibility of beliefs above all other values or beliefs. Placing a premium on establishing and maintaining flexibility and openness in family beliefs creates important family freedoms for all. Flexibility and openness inevitably enhance the common good and social justice in families, communities, and societies. When the flexibility of family beliefs is a goal in building personal relationships, or in parenting, the outcomes of these interactions produce mature and independent adults, who are both genuinely respectful and realistically concerned about each other's well-being. Achieving flexibility in family beliefs improves civilizations, because these socially intelligent ways of thinking, being, and acting increase freedom.

Flexible family beliefs are maintained as long as families permit and encourage their members to question their own family beliefs and family values. Questioning in these families is not the privilege of a few elders, or an allowed activity for adults only, but rather a way of life that is followed by all family members. Because learning plays a crucial role in families with flexible belief systems, these families use their relatives' questions to achieve deeper kinds of learning, as well as to review what they think they know, and what they should do.

Formulating the most significant questions to ask each other is common in families with flexible beliefs. These families are willing to revise their everyday ways of seeing things and doing things, in order to be more inclusive in how they interact and work together as families. Families with flexible beliefs are more open to criticisms, in principle, so they create a stronger common good in their families and in societies. Because of these achievements, family members respect the value of learning about their situations, and the continuous questioning in families with flexible beliefs becomes a way of life. This shared habit, in families with flexible beliefs, allows their family members to collect many facts, so that they make more enlightened decisions to promote family and social conditions that encourage freedom and autonomy.

In sum, because families are the most significant social sources of our beliefs, it is important to recognize that it is particularly families with flexible beliefs that are more socially intelligent, and more able to truly support their members. Families with flexible beliefs are necessarily more open than families with rigid beliefs, which, by contrast, tend to have relatively closed emotional relationships. However, members of families with rigid beliefs continuously improve their conditions and circumstances, especially if they change their families so that they accept and create more flexible beliefs. Increasing social intelligence is a reliable strategy to accomplish this, which benefits family members as well as societies.

Changing Family Beliefs

From the point of view of social intelligence, the primary purpose of defining our beliefs, as well as tracing their social origins, is to determine whether or not we are living according to those beliefs that we cherish the most. In many obvious and subtle ways, we tend to absorb and act on beliefs which we have not yet made our own. In fact, sometimes we internalize beliefs, or even entire belief systems, which are alien to our real beliefs and interests, or which contradict our deepest principles. When such anomalies occur, we find ourselves in constant conflict with others as well as with ourselves, and our energies are unnecessarily depleted. This means that we cannot be as effective in our actions as we want to be.

When we do not have well-coordinated beliefs, or beliefs that we are aware of, we should clarify our starting points by assessing where we stand in relation to beliefs that we have absorbed throughout our lives to the present. This is a major task, and it is essential to do this if we are to succeed in changing our beliefs. For example, we need to clarify what our current beliefs really are, as well as what we want our most dominant beliefs to be, if we are to increase our social intelligence.

This process of clarification begins when we are aware of the roles our beliefs play in our actions, as well as how our beliefs originated and developed in our exchanges with family members and others throughout our lives. Even though it is helpful to single out particular individuals, usually family members, who seem to have influenced us the most, it is often those people with whom we have interacted the most whose beliefs we accepted as our own. Thus our mundane, everyday patterns of family interactions frequently affect us more deeply than our sporadic exchanges with authorities we sought out expressly to guide our decisions and actions.

Changing our family beliefs, so that we increase our social intelligence and work toward social justice, begins by examining the substance of our beliefs, as well as the different ways we interact with relatives who influenced—and still influence—our beliefs. Focusing on the priority of increasing our social intelligence by changing our family beliefs is essential, because beliefs absorbed from our families are usually our most deep-seated and most difficult-to-change beliefs.

Beliefs we took from our families, which include beliefs about families, are lodged at the heart of our being, because they are laden with emotions from our family dependencies. Our families are emotional relationship systems, and we often accept specific beliefs due to the facts of our situations in these

15

emotional relationships. Because of the importance of understanding the family sources of our beliefs, sorting out what our beliefs mean is extraordinarily complex. We proceed most effectively by identifying patterns in our family interactions which transmitted particular beliefs to us through time, as well as through the different generations of our families.

Even though our goals are to assess the impacts of our families' beliefs on our social intelligence, it is useful to examine how we acquired particular beliefs from our parents, grandparents, and siblings—or whoever the key players are in our family interactions through time. Compiling family histories helps us to accomplish this, so that we understand more fully those patterns of dominance that existed in our families during our most dependent years, as well as patterns that continue to the present. For example, who made decisions about whether or not we were raised in particular religions? Who led our families in deciding which religious observances our families would conduct? Who were the family members who decided how we were socialized into our religious beliefs, including those who brought pressures to bear on our conformity to selected rituals and practices?

These explorations of our families' beliefs start to change some of our own relatively dysfunctional family beliefs. Our increased clarity about our beliefs allows us to better establish a unified set of beliefs, which will serve us more efficiently and more effectively. We also increasingly appreciate the subtlety of the social nature of our beliefs, at deeper levels of our being, so that we are more in charge of what we do and what we want to accomplish on a daily basis. Once we make some deliberate changes in beliefs which derive from our families, we begin to change how we relate to others in varied social settings.

In sum, being socially intelligent means that we let go of our unproductive beliefs, so that we can embrace beliefs that we truly choose and honor. Ideally, when we relinquish our less meaningful beliefs, we automatically absorb beliefs that ring more true, because we are increasingly aware and mature in our responses to others. When we decide which beliefs we want to nurture, we act more closely in accordance with our chosen beliefs. Ultimately, changing our family beliefs means that we deliberately select the major directions in our lives, so that we are more in charge of our destinies.

Above all, we change our beliefs most effectively by changing our actions. When we interact with those who inspire us, for example, we select goals which transcend negative realities in our everyday situations. Furthermore, because of the increased significance of our actions, we live ourselves into new beliefs, which adds purpose and direction to dealing with our daily challenges. However, these new beliefs must not become fixed or static. We need to remain sufficiently aware of all our family beliefs, for example, so that we can again let go of beliefs that hold us back. At the same time, we choose to strengthen those family beliefs that support the accomplishment of our most cherished goals.

Nurturing Social Justice
Understanding new possibilities and innovative ways to change our beliefs starts with examining our beliefs, and deciding which beliefs we want to nurture. However, because our individual well-being depends largely on the welfare and interdependence of a wide range of different groups—from small groups, such as families, to mass conglomerations, like international communities—we have to consider what our responsibilities are in relation to broad social contexts and varied social conditions.

Although the specific ways in which we contribute to societies may contrast sharply with what others do, depending on our experiences and inclinations, in principle we need to accept that we have the power to influence the overall qualities of life in our societies. This means that it is both appropriate and useful to at least ponder how we can improve the well-being of the greatest number of people in those small groups and populations to which we belong.

The existential issues involved in considering what social justice is, and how we can increase social justice, are critical concerns in our decision-making about which beliefs we should cultivate and nurture in the long run. Our social intelligence shows us that our beliefs are essentially both intended and unintended consequences of our interactions with others, most particularly our family interactions. Given these facts, we have to decide how we can make sense of our biological and moral imperatives to live fully, by contributing to societies, as well as to our own needs and the needs of our families. For example, what priority should be given to social justice in the total scheme of our concerns, time, and energies?

Only when we see that our own well-being is inextricably connected to the well-being of others, do we understand that unless we choose to nurture social justice, the conditions of our existence will ultimately be undermined. Social intelligence helps us to understand our necessary and critical interconnectedness, and motivates us to continue to increase our social intelligence, in order to bring social justice to different groups and societies.

Social justice is essentially a set of meaningful ideals. Social justice creates increased opportunities to share some of the dividends that social intelligence brings, and to design reliable ways to ensure that the world will thrive constructively rather than be destroyed. Unless our common good is shared by all, for example, predictable negative repercussions will be experienced by each one of us, including members of our international communities. Because we have changed from living in relatively small societies to being global societies, our commitments to social justice are even more crucial and more necessary today than in the past.

With regard to our family beliefs, and the ways in which our family beliefs influence what we do, we must first of all

18

appreciate that our ultimate goals in life should not be to increase the well-being of only our families. Although meeting our families' real needs continues to be essential, this is not only what we should do with our lives. In order to live fully, we need to aim to accomplish personal and social goals or objectives which transcend the immediate press of individual and family needs. Our solutions to our varied situations are to turn outward to embrace and resolve issues which affect the world's needs, especially by nurturing and increasing social justice.

We increase social justice most effectively when we know ourselves, and our families, sufficiently well to be able to direct some of our talents and energies toward particular aspects of social justice. For example, when we consider our shared needs for more egalitarian relationships in the world, or for more equal distributions of resources, we find meaningful directions to take. Similarly, when we consider widespread needs for inclusive communities, or for more diverse communities, we see how resolutions based on social justice bring about constructive changes. Pondering the advantages of cooperation and openness in families, and in societies, helps us to appreciate the fact that the qualities of our social bonds increase social justice.

One of the first questions to ask ourselves, in considering how we can nurture social justice today, is how we and our families can best care for those in need, so that their lives will be as rewarding as our own. Furthermore, for pragmatic reasons, we cannot afford to turn our backs on others' needs and concerns, because at the same time this makes us vulnerable to their dissatisfaction and unrest about being unable to lead satisfying lives. We need to assume some responsibilities for those who do not have our advantages and privileges, and at the same time share our awareness of the social realities we all face, so that both we and they participate more fully in resolving our shared social issues and mutual concerns.

II. Religions

For many people, their beliefs about life are closely related to their religious beliefs. However, individuals and families are often more aware of their particular religious beliefs, than they are of their general, everyday beliefs and assumptions. For example, religious beliefs are thought of as clear ways to distinguish individuals and families from other members of their local communities or societies. Thus, our religious beliefs and our identities are usually more strongly connected, and more salient in our decision-making, than our secular beliefs and our identities.

In many respects, we learn our first secular belief systems at the same time that we absorb our religious beliefs—often through similar but less ritualized patterns of family interactions. Although we are not usually as aware that our secular rituals and practices are related to our secular beliefs, in the same direct ways that our religious rituals express our religious beliefs, social intelligence shows us that we are similarly guided by our families' interactions in formulating and practicing our political or scientific beliefs. In addition, patterns in family and community exchanges influence which secular beliefs we accept, and which secular leaders we follow.

Other important characteristics of our religious beliefs are that they are often introduced to us when we are very young and impressionable, as well as presented to us as clusters of beliefs or belief systems. Our religious identities are not formed through the interventions of prophets or supreme beings, but rather through our shared participation in the beliefs and rituals of the particular religions practiced in our families. Consequently, it is especially the beliefs and practices of the religious leaders of our families that have the most profound influences on how we understand religions in general, as well as our family religions.

We learn how to be Christians, Jews, or Muslims by practicing or observing distinctive beliefs, rituals, and life cycle celebrations. In Western societies it is considered unusual, or even deviant, to identify with more than one religion. In the West, we consider that our commitments are deeper when we practice only one religion, because this means that other religious beliefs will not contradict or nullify each other. By contrast, in Eastern societies, several religions are more likely to be practiced by the same individuals or families.

Families' religions and practices are integral parts of their emotional systems, especially where similar patterns of beliefs and rituals are repeated through several generations. We frequently become religious if at least one of our relatives believes that a particular religious world view is valuable, because it makes a real difference in how we perceive ourselves and others, as well as in how we define our individual and social responsibilities. Thus hierarchies of religious beliefs tend to become significant aspects of our overall faiths, rather than scientific or closely reasoned rationales about human existence. Furthermore, we often believe in our religions because they give us important rewards, such as strong identities, solace, reassurance, meaning, and community membership.

Religious beliefs have similar variations to our family beliefs. We and our families have a few basic religious beliefs, for example, which are frequently shared, even by people who are not in our families, and who may identify with contrasting religious traditions. By extension, when individuals aim to be spiritual, rather than religious, they frequently develop selected basic religious beliefs that represent common denominators among several different religious traditions. For example, Christians, Muslims, and Jews increase their possibilities for achieving interfaith spirituality, when they base their interactions and communications on wisdom literatures that emphasize what their religions share, rather than how they contrast with each other.

Religious beliefs are also unique with respect to specific religions. Different religious traditions have distinctive approaches to defining supreme deities, religious practices, world views, assumptions about human nature, possibilities for spiritual development, and rituals for life cycle events. These unique aspects of religions distinguish them from other religions, and may become indirect means to assess the strength of individuals' commitments to particular religious beliefs. For example, members of a religion who honor only a few, rather than most of a religion's beliefs and practices, are sometimes thought to be less religious for doing so.

As in understanding families' beliefs, religious beliefs may be rigid or flexible. Although some religious believers value the strictness of their adherence to particular principles of their beliefs and practices, this rigidity usually narrows or even harms how they accomplish tasks, especially with regard to family relations, social relations, and secular adaptations. By contrast, some degree of flexibility in commitments to religious beliefs breathes life into family relations, social relations, and secular adaptations. Therefore, partly depending on religious authorities or religious sanctions used in family interactions, rigid and flexible religious beliefs have contrasting outcomes for family members' everyday behavior.

Religious beliefs are frequently difficult to change because they are built on non-rational commitments, and may have been transmitted—at early, impressionable ages—through several generations in the same families. When religious beliefs are successfully internalized as young children, for example, it may be particularly problematic to find effective ways to change such deep-seated orientations, even as mature adults.

Social intelligence helps us to modify our religious beliefs, so that we deal with our everyday trials and tribulations more meaningfully and more effectively. We may need to decide, for example, whether we are more committed to honoring our family's long-standing family religious traditions, or to accepting the spouse of an adult child who is not a member of our family's religion. In this situation, social intelligence shows us how to find dependable ways to prioritize our own and others' religious beliefs, so that we can both cherish our own religious beliefs and deal thoughtfully with complex, modern, social situations such as interfaith marriages.

Many traditional religions incorporate social justice principles in their beliefs. Social intelligence helps us to find those religious beliefs, values, world views, and traditions which best address social justice issues. When we go in this direction, we learn that there is no existential dilemma in choosing between practicing particular religions, and working toward social justice. Rather, some of us deliberately search for ways to combine our interests in social justice with specific religious traditions, principles, or practices.

An effective starting point, for achieving these syntheses, is to focus on basic religious beliefs, and to consider what the common denominators of different religious traditions are. For example, we may work together more effectively, when we are from different religious traditions, if we concentrate on our shared beliefs in spirituality. Although spiritual practices often derive from specific religious principles, spirituality can also be thought of as bringing social justice to our everyday situations, including global outreach.

Basic Religious Beliefs

Religious beliefs view the world in ways that honor and privilege powers that go beyond our human or social capacities.

II. Religions

Religions encourage us to depend on supernatural powers, which are greater than human beings, because we know that harmful consequences can flow from our human frailties and human errors. Religious beliefs revere God, or supernatural powers, which are unattainable by humans, based on realizations that our modern and secular worlds are not solely the result of knowable human actions.

Religious awe for the complexity and power of energies in the universe, both personal and impersonal, often gives us a sense of powerlessness over significant aspects of our lives and destinies. This does not mean that we are not in control of certain aspects of our actions, but rather that the invisible, unknowable influences that surround us are extremely powerful in our everyday situations and challenges.

As well as encouraging a strong sense of awe about the wonders and fearful powers of the universe, religious beliefs—at both personal and social levels—can motivate us to accomplish particular objectives, especially when our actions are dedicated to a religious purpose which transcends our own selfish interests. Religious beliefs also help us to withstand setbacks, so that we can make long term efforts and lasting commitments, thereby being more effective in whatever we do.

Different religious traditions encourage particular beliefs and attitudes toward our relatives or strangers. The moral codes that many of us learn in childhood, for example, derive from our basic religious beliefs. Similarly, our basic religious beliefs encourage particular postures to building relationships with others, which often become invaluable guides in how to behave. Given these possible uses of our basic religious beliefs, our social intelligence helps us to determine to what extent these beliefs provide us with beneficial orientations to life.

Our religions may be tremendously significant sources of our basic beliefs about human nature. However, even though we understand this fact intellectually, we often have considerable difficulty in changing those of our religious beliefs that do not allow us to accomplish our ideals or goals. For example, our religious beliefs—even when held in high regard for sacred purposes—may not consistently guide us to develop our potentials as human beings.

Social intelligence encourages us to examine our basic religious beliefs together with what we consider to be the highest purposes of our lives. When we are socially intelligent, we are aware of how social conditions surrounding our religious beliefs have influenced our beliefs, as well as the extent to which social pressures—rather than divine imperatives—affect what we decide to do on a daily basis. Social intelligence suggests ways to assess the extent to which our religious beliefs are religious, social, or political, and how these social spheres or social systems overlap. Social intelligence also challenges us to combine our religious and social concerns in our enlightened considerations of what it means to do God's will, or to increase social justice on a daily basis.

When we review what we consider to be our basic religious and basic secular beliefs, we realize the many ways in which our beliefs influence the totality of our lives. For example, we often cross busy streets safely due to the beliefs we hold, just as the extent to which we live our lives fully depends on the beliefs we have. We may not accomplish either of these tasks successfully, however, unless we choose beliefs which make our actions both possible and effective. Furthermore, our choices among different beliefs are clearer and more enlightened when we know what our basic religious and secular beliefs are.

Our basic religious beliefs are usually more difficult to resist or change than our unique religious beliefs. This is because our basic religious beliefs are developed at deeper emotional levels of our being, and they are often more readily applied to our everyday situations than our unique religious beliefs. The degree of fixedness of our basic religious beliefs may be problematic, although when we make even slight shifts in our basic religious beliefs, we open up substantial opportunities and options to live differently.

Sometimes our religious beliefs seem to clash with our secular beliefs and modern realities. We may need to find ways to increase the meaningfulness of our commitments to our basic religious beliefs, while at the same time pursuing secular goals, such as social justice. Social intelligence helps us to reconcile our needs to both move with the times, and maintain our roots in particular religious traditions. We discover, for example, that we can honor the basic religious beliefs of our religious heritages, as well as benefit from their assurances of support, when we pursue secular goals. Believing in progressive revelations in all religious traditions enables us to pursue social justice amidst modern secular pressures, so that our acts of social justice deepen our appreciation and experiences of our ongoing religious revelations.

Unique Religious Beliefs

Even though we usually think of ourselves as sharing all or most of the religious beliefs and practices of people who are affiliated with our particular religion, in reality many variations in religious beliefs and practices exist among members of identical denominational or sectarian religions, as well as among family members who belong to the same religion. In some respects variations in beliefs and practices within the same religious denominations, or among different religious sects in the same religions, may be almost as great as variations among completely different religions. This is especially so when individual religions are polarized between traditional and modern interpretations of religious beliefs, or between highly organized or relatively unorganized religious communities and practices.

For our purposes of increasing our social intelligence through understanding the social sources of our religious beliefs, it is sufficient to acknowledge that individual and social variations in religious beliefs and practices are inevitable, and often desirable. We are not automatons, and this variability allows us sufficient leeway to develop our own understanding and practices of religions. However, it also means that we cannot speak meaningfully about religious experiences with one voice, but rather look for patterns among varied religious beliefs and practices. Both our subjective impressions and objective facts validate our interpretations of how our religious and secular beliefs affect what we do every day.

Our unique religious beliefs are a necessary reality for understanding our religious practices, and an important dimension of the social sources of our religious beliefs. For instance, we may attribute the uniqueness of our religious beliefs to our individual experiences of religion, particularly because of specific patterns of family interaction that influenced how we were introduced to our families' religions and religious practices. In addition to family variations in acquiring our religious beliefs, we have choices among the intrinsic contrasts in values and world views offered by each organized religion.

In some respects hierarchies of beliefs and values in religions encourage insider unity, as well as insider-outsider or outsider-insider antagonisms among their members, especially with respect to other religions or other societies. Even though some of the basic religious beliefs of many religions may be to tolerate, appreciate, and peacefully co-exist with other religions, some unique religious beliefs may encourage petty or serious conflicts among religions. When differences among unique religious beliefs become too polarized, they may eventually lead to extremely destructive behavior and wars.

History shows us that potentially destructive differences, among unique religious beliefs, negate some of the benefits of enrichment gained by experiencing contrasts in religious beliefs. Thus clinging unconditionally to unique religious beliefs may become dangerous for all concerned. In this respect,

II. Religions

social intelligence requires us to be as level-headed as possible in assessing the advantages and disadvantages of our unique religious beliefs, so that we do not unknowingly create unnecessarily destructive consequences or lethal schisms.

Whereas a quest to find common denominators among basic religious beliefs predictably leads us toward meaningful compromises among religions, or toward building communities of peaceful coexistence with other believers, pursuing unique religious beliefs may divert our attention from increasing social justice. Because our religious beliefs and practices are built largely on emotional foundations, we must make sure that our religious faiths are not blind to their social causes or social consequences. We cannot afford to wrap ourselves in security blankets of unique religious beliefs and practices, because doing so risks bringing about destructive consequences such as increasing ethnocentrism, prejudice, and discrimination.

Social intelligence is a reliable guide for making vital assessments of the extent to which our religious beliefs focus on basic religious beliefs, which can more easily be shared or used in the give-and-take of everyday life, or unique religious beliefs, which may potentially divide people and lead to destruction. In making these assessments we must ask ourselves whether the beliefs and values of life, or the beliefs and values of death, should dominate our lives, as well as what these polarities mean in today's complex modern world.

When we choose to create a viable global community for the future, social intelligence is a rich resource to help us to understand how our religious beliefs contribute to this goal. Social intelligence also helps us to face and deal with important issues. For example, should our everyday decisions be based on our assessments of good and evil, which may be ambiguous, or on our religious beliefs? How can we formulate the most practical plans possible to preserve or ensure our civilizations and freedom, through both our basic and unique religious beliefs?

Rigid Religious Beliefs

One of the distinguishing characteristics of both basic and unique religious beliefs is that we endow them with transcendental powers. To the extent that religious beliefs include definitions of supernatural beings, or forces that supersede human nature, religious beliefs are exceedingly more powerful than beliefs about the everyday realities of mere mortals. Religious beliefs, including the awesome force of religious sanctions, persistently wield strong influences over human choices, decisions, and world views.

Rigid religious beliefs, whether they are essentially basic religious beliefs or unique religious beliefs, are particularly coercive in their regulation of the actions of individuals, families, communities, and societies. When believers are afraid of being subjected to the fires of hell or eternal damnation, for example, they are particularly cautious about how they behave with respect to honoring religious laws. In fact, because complete lifetimes can be regulated in this way, sometimes neither individuals nor groups dare raise questions about whether they have real choices in how they behave. Apprehensive tensions increase the power of rigid religious beliefs. For example, religious believers tend to do what is expected of them, because they fear the consequences of disobeying the religious dictates of family members or others who have rigid religious beliefs.

Rigid religious beliefs have the advantage of giving clarity to religious leaders and their communities of believers. However, this clarity is bought at the cost of accuracy, with the result that valuable human energies are perpetually sacrificed in the name of religious faiths. In these situations, family interactions, and other social exchanges, become unduly influenced by family members' rigid religious beliefs. Social intelligence helps us to determine where human errors lie in understanding these complex situations, even when there is considerable agreement among relatives that some family members' rigid interpretations of God's will are false.

II. Religions

Although a family member's rigid religious beliefs are intrinsically difficult for other relatives to deal with, it is particularly their supernatural sanctions that make rigid religious beliefs both forceful and coercive in their power and impacts. Social intelligence helps us to find meaningful answers to important questions, such as how to interpret the principles of particular religious beliefs. How much influence should individual family members have in their assessments of what is right or wrong? To what extent do traditional religions give us viable guidelines for navigating our complicated modern societies? How is the ideal of social justice tied into, or excluded from, those rigid religious beliefs that influence us the most?

When we explore how we were influenced by rigid religious beliefs in our families, education, and politics, we examine how particular leaders passed on their rigid religious beliefs to us, and the consequences that these rigid religious beliefs have for our everyday decision-making. Social intelligence suggests that to the extent that our responses and adaptations to rigid religious beliefs yield satisfactory results, there may be no real reason to discard them, as long as we understand and modify their most destructive social characteristics and consequences.

Social intelligence compels us to exercise whatever courage is necessary to ask deep questions about these issues, so that we can act with enlightenment, rather than merely reinvent worlds according to how we wish they were. Social intelligence rests on the premise that there are predictabilities in our social universes that must be understood and respected, and that wisdom literatures have developed some important deep and comprehensive understanding of patterns in our religious beliefs and traditions. However, we need to take the power of our relatively new, modern, secular societies into consideration, as well as contemporary social conditions in our global communities. Our goal should be to deal with issues raised by social justice ideals, rather than to play with the toys and baubles that capitalism and industrialization provide.

Social intelligence guides us to make these assessments and value choices. Even though, conceivably, the content of rigid religious beliefs may increase the common good and social justice, as well as add clarity to our thinking, when we understand more fully how religious beliefs can be used for constructive purposes, we realize that dogma and bigotry have no place in any society. The stakes for human survival, through successful adaptations to modern social conditions, are too high for us to risk living in accordance with the narrow, partial world views of rigid religious beliefs. It is even more imperative today, than ever before, that we learn how to cultivate social justice collectively, so that we can open up opportunities for everyone in our global communities, as well as cultivate a truly global common good.

Flexible Religious Beliefs

Both rigid and flexible religious beliefs derive from established denominational religions or religious sects. However, flexible religious beliefs are considerably more open-ended, as well as more critical or questioning in posture, than rigid religious beliefs. Because all religions are social products, rather than divine entities, flexible religious beliefs are perpetually modified through both individual and group actions. However, whereas we generally seek to change our flexible religious beliefs, we more often resist changing our rigid religious beliefs.

Rigid religious beliefs are usually based on the principle that divine revelation occurs at particular times in history or at only one point in time. The centrality of this belief in the historically specific revelations of rigid religious beliefs limits possibilities for new interpretations or changes within these religions, as well as possibilities for continuing progressive revelations. By contrast, flexible religious beliefs expressly emerge from the continuous questioning of religious beliefs, and there are explicit assumptions in flexible religious beliefs that divine revelations can and will occur in the present and future, as well as in the past.

Flexible religious beliefs support possibilities for wide variations, including contradictions, among the many individual or group interpretations of religious traditions. Although this tolerance does not necessarily encourage the creation of new religions, such as haphazard or thoughtless combinations of several religious traditions, broader applications of religious principles are usually made in flexible religious beliefs than in rigid religious beliefs.

Social intelligence shows us that useful questions to ask about flexible religious beliefs include specifications and clarifications concerning the nature of God and spirituality, definitions of God's will for people in traditional or modern societies, and assumptions relating to human possibilities or limitations. Social intelligence also draws attention to familial and broad social dimensions of flexible religious beliefs, with their implications for human experiences, rather than solely to the content of flexible religious beliefs.

Flexible religious beliefs safeguard us in times of crisis, because they do not depend on fixed religious rituals to deal with significant turning points in our lives. They encourage us to use our knowledge and experiences as guides for our decisions and actions, at the same time that we seriously explore answers that our religious traditions give us concerning our current situations. For example, flexible religious beliefs suggest that God's will for us can be thought of as a synthesis of traditional religious beliefs, our everyday awareness of God, our surrender and commitments to Spirit, and our openness to new possibilities for responsible actions.

Flexible religious beliefs help us to continue to make changes and adaptations in our religious beliefs, so that we can deal more effectively with whatever happens in our lives. Our social intelligence ensures that we do not become trapped in the inevitable time warps of rigid religious beliefs, with their overly narrow ready-made answers to ongoing human dilemmas. Furthermore, when we are guided by flexible religious beliefs, we no longer look backward in time to traditional religious sources for answers, as we do when we use more rigid religious beliefs.

Social intelligence encourages us to be thoughtful and critical about the degree of flexibility we allow into our religious beliefs. However, when we are socially intelligent, we do not depend on personal, idiosyncratic versions of religion. Instead social intelligence encourages enlightened, informed decisions about which established religious beliefs serve us best, as we continue to test and redefine all things sacred and profane through our lived experiences. Overall we compare, for example, the quality of our lives with flexible religious beliefs, and our lives without flexible religious beliefs. Similarly, we test out the effectiveness of the adjustments we make in using flexible religious beliefs to guide our actions, such as combining our understanding of increasing social justice with our understanding of doing God's will.

Even though social intelligence has an avowedly secular orientation to existential issues, being aware of the social dimensions of flexible religious beliefs helps us to put religions and wisdom literatures in perspective. We face the possibility that we might miss important aspects of civilization, for example, if we turn our backs on religious beliefs. Absorbing flexible religious beliefs increases meaning and purpose in our lives, as well as direction, and we increasingly benefit from the most spiritually enlightened sources and creations that have emerged in different times and places. By cultivating flexible religious beliefs, we apply deliberately selected religious principles in our everyday lives, thereby preserving some of our most meaningful religious traditions.

Changing Religious Beliefs
There are many different directions in which our religious beliefs can be changed, as well as many ways to change our

religious beliefs. Religious beliefs are important beyond our individual preferences, because they are significant influences in societies. Thus some of the mechanisms of changing our religious beliefs may seem to be outside the control of individual believers. There are critical masses of believers within religious denominations, for example, which may dominate other religions and religious beliefs in a particular society or societies.

These facts about religions' statuses frequently give dominant religions leadership roles in societal and global changes in religious and secular beliefs. However, widespread tensions between religious beliefs and major social influences like modernization and secularization also exist. Against this backdrop of broad shifts in the structures and attitudes of populations, social intelligence helps us to see that particular religious beliefs may become less important to both societies and individuals. This broader picture of religions and religious beliefs is a strong influence on the impact religions have on individual and social conditions in societies and global communities.

Thus history directly affects the scope and dimensions of our religious beliefs. Even though we may already feel that our religions are not entirely our own, because of the ways in which we were socialized into our religions by our families, social intelligence reminds us that broad social influences in societies also affect the types and qualities of our religious beliefs. One of our existential challenges, in determining what we believe, is that we need to explore how social influences around our religions—as well as within our religions—have affected and still influence our ongoing choices of religious beliefs and practices.

These complexities in our religious beliefs also require us to carefully assess our real choices in religious beliefs, so that they are effective guides for our daily behavior, as well as ways to direct our formal religious affiliations and devotional practices.

We cannot afford to take our religious beliefs for granted by acting automatically, because our choices in religious beliefs are powerful influences on the outcomes of our actions. The more we stay alert to the social dimensions and social realities of our possibilities, for example, the more productive we become in accomplishing what it is that means the most to us.

In the same ways that we change family beliefs that contradict or neutralize what we really believe—or what we really want to do—in order to be more socially intelligent, we must become aware of what our weakest and most problematic religious beliefs are as soon as we can. This requires focus and direct action, so that we can effectively let go of whatever troubles us the most. However, because religious beliefs play such a critical role in defining our world views, as well as our particular situations, changing our religious beliefs may be easier when we focus on only one or two of our already established beliefs to orient our behavior and practices.

Selecting one or two of our beliefs to apply to our lives gives us new or deeper sources of meaning, purpose, and direction in orienting our everyday actions. For example, even though we may feel that we have already acted in accordance with our beliefs in the existence of God, singling out this particular belief encourages us to meditate more deeply on what God is, and to show ourselves how believing in God is followed by marked differences in our decision-making, and in establishing our daily priorities. These changes expand our possibilities for identifying and defining opportunities to work effectively toward accomplishing our most cherished goals.

Trial and error actions clarify which religious beliefs we need to let go of, and which we need to hold close. Even though there are myriad variations and ramifications of meditating and acting on a high or the highest priority of believing in God, changing our priorities necessarily transforms our lives, especially when our belief in God becomes more central in what we do. Although this is not our only choice for an effective starting point in assessing our religious beliefs, it can be an initial way to assess and refine what we really believe.

If the advantages of having a dependable belief in God are not clear, another starting point is to temporarily put all our religious beliefs to one side, so that we can consider the universe from perspectives of nonbelievers or atheists. If we want to make radical changes in our religious beliefs, these more secular perspectives should be tried and tested, until there is some personal evidence of what is right for us, or of whether religious beliefs can guide us.

Social intelligence helps us to increase our objectivity in making these significant assessments and choices about changing our religious beliefs. Applying social intelligence to our religious beliefs makes us more aware of the complexities of social influences in our religious experiences, so that we can make more enlightened and more responsible choices about our religious beliefs. Social intelligence also helps us to consider the role of social justice in expressing our religious or nonreligious beliefs.

Nurturing Social Justice
In spite of the often widespread feelings that there are no real purposes to our existence, it appears that we do at least have choices between opposing purposes—like living in directions that take us closer to achieving social justice, and living in ways that ultimately bring about social annihilation. Although we have options other than these polarities—for example, we could dissipate our energies by going to and fro with contradictory random actions—we often tend to move toward one of these main ends or the other. Given our existential imperatives to survive, many of us deliberately choose to preserve civilizations, or at least to maintain reasonable living conditions for as many people as possible, especially if we believe that the opposite choices—of social destruction—are real.

Because religions have historically helped us to understand our complex social and moral dilemmas throughout the ages, some religious sources of wisdom may enlighten us to ways of solving social justice issues. As a result of our own considerable misunderstanding and confusion in applying particular survival and fulfillment strategies to our own lives, we realize that we benefit from clarifying and simplifying the stakes in deciding what we do with our own lives. For example, we may assess the extent to which we find meaning in our everyday routines, or how interested we are in making the world a better place for ourselves and coming generations.

In recent times, some people consider working toward increasing social justice as an alternative to living according to traditional religious beliefs and practices. However, we do not yet have effective ways to inspire sufficient numbers of believers from different religious traditions to work together cooperatively for long periods of time, in order to address and attain similar shared goals. Developing spirituality, for example, often seems too remote from history and human suffering, unless doing God's will is considered to be synonymous with increasing social justice. In these respects, living for the purpose of achieving social justice may become a moral equivalent of doing God's will.

Whatever rationale people attribute to pursuing social justice in our complex modern societies, there is no doubt that having this objective can add meaning, purpose, and direction to individuals' decisions and actions on a daily basis. This also suggests that nurturing the goal of achieving social justice, is a worthwhile responsibility, especially in light of the considerable ongoing conflicts and suffering in today's world.

Ideally, nurturing social justice goes beyond personal and private decision-making and actions, to include public works. Because ultimately we need to act collectively to achieve social justice, we must make our own positions on social issues known, if we are to organize effectively along these lines. Just as we gain comfort and support from worshipping in traditional religious communities, we benefit from sharing our beliefs in the necessity for social justice when we enter into public discourse. Furthermore, because many varied steps have to be taken to achieve social justice, maintaining some of our religious motivations may be crucial, in that they help us to stay on track when inevitable difficulties arise in our efforts to reach our goals.

Thus some religious beliefs and perspectives help us to clarify social justice issues. Because religions have historically given us reasons to continue to exist, these resources may be invaluable for taking on lifetime commitments to social justice. Religious beliefs and social justice often overlap comfortably, so that religious beliefs can be drawn upon in order to achieve coherence and coordination in our social justice ideals and actions. This posture and orientation defines the content of our social justice concerns, and fuels the energies we need to stay the course.

Although associations between religious beliefs and social justice may imply that social justice is best achieved through using both basic religious beliefs and flexible religious beliefs, this is not necessarily so. Working toward social justice, and heightening our awareness about social justice, may also flow from softening some of the narrowness and rigidity of our unique religious or secular beliefs. When we apply our religious beliefs to solving critical social problems, we at the same time necessarily work toward accomplishing the broader secular goal of achieving social justice more effectively. Consequently, having this kind of comprehensive objective consolidates the efforts of people who have varied religious beliefs, so that even the uniqueness and rigidity of their religious beliefs may sustain their collective efforts to meet their shared goals or ideals of social justice.

To the extent that social justice transcends contrasts in our religious beliefs, it may also change our religious beliefs. We become different people through our actions, so that working to increase social justice may ultimately transform our religious beliefs, as well as our identities. Social intelligence helps us to understand these processes more deeply, and guides our critical decision-making. These enhanced capacities are vital for keeping us on track sufficiently to reach our socially intelligent goals.

III. Social Classes

Our beliefs serve many personal and social purposes. To the extent that we live in fairly privileged social situations, we tend to merely enjoy our beliefs, without being concerned about what their functions or consequences are. For example, beliefs characteristically add zest to our daily lives, especially when they motivate us to pursue chosen goals, or to do work that we enjoy. Furthermore, religious beliefs may give us broad views of a meaningful universe and our roles in it. At best, the sum total of our beliefs provides meaning, purpose, and direction in our daily activities.

In a more objective, concrete sense, our beliefs accompany and uphold social institutions, such as social classes, so that society can be organized with a greater degree of order and predictability. Because people do not usually benefit from being in low status social classes, there may be considerable tension between what we think our social classes are, and how others see us. However, in spite of our best efforts to define our own social class memberships, we are both in the classes we think we are in, as well as in classes considered appropriate by those who may label us differently.

In any event, social classes, and the beliefs they engender, frequently have a tremendously strong influence on our lives without our realizing it. For example, we may be confined by our own beliefs about expectations associated with particular social classes, or we may be restricted by others' beliefs about our social classes. Although we are sometimes mistaken in our assessments of what these social class expectations are, or about the power of others' beliefs, it is nevertheless difficult to escape the influences of the obvious or imperceptible aspects of our beliefs in social classes.

One of the reasons we find it challenging to neutralize the impacts of our beliefs in social classes, is that social classes apply to different aspects of our lives in addition to our material assets. For example, we may be members of specific social classes because of our religious beliefs, genders, sexual orientations, races, ethnicities, ablebodiedness, or health.

Our many different social class systems interact with each other and influence our beliefs, well-being, and behavior. However, the pervasiveness of our shared capacities to organize ourselves into hierarchies, to classify others as well as ourselves, and to accept traditional ways of thinking about social classes make our beliefs about social classes both widespread and deep-seated. In modern times, we are ever-ready to categorize ourselves and others according to a wide range of selected social differences.

Another reason that makes our beliefs in social classes difficult to escape is the degree of subtlety with which social class meanings are communicated in our everyday exchanges. We express social class signals to others, often without realizing it, so that our ordinary ways of relating to people reinforce our complex social class differences. At the same time, we try to maintain our social honor in these exchanges, partly by implicitly ranking ourselves in relation to others, even when we enter into the simplest of interactions.

These customary patterns of behavior derive largely from our beliefs in social class differences. Furthermore, our beliefs in social classes legitimate the personal and social functions of class differences. This means that we cannot dismiss our beliefs in social classes as superficial, or as figments of our imaginations. We believe in the existence and characteristics of social classes, at least to some extent, with the result that we perpetuate social classes from generation to generation. In addition, social classes have strong impacts on what we do, because we fuel social class realities with intensely emotional individual and shared beliefs about social classes.

Social intelligence helps us to see the social origins of our beliefs in social classes, as well as the social functions and purposes that social class beliefs perform for individuals, communities, and societies. However, we are not fatalistically destined to particular life outcomes because we are members of specific social classes, even though our beliefs in social classes may predispose us to unnecessarily narrow our life options and chances.

Applying social intelligence to social class issues gives us more objectivity about our particular situations, so that we see more clearly how some of our beliefs in social classes hold us back by limiting our opportunities. Social intelligence also helps us to locate new possibilities, which essentially neutralize the negative effects of our social class positions and expectations. When we become more objective about our social classes, we act more directly or more efficiently to achieve social justice, and to increase the common good.

Basic Social Class Beliefs

Social classes produce all the structures and processes needed to replicate themselves. Consequently, our beliefs in social classes are self-propagated. In this context, our basic social class beliefs are the most deep-seated of our beliefs about social classes, as well as those beliefs which are the most widely shared among populations with the same or different social class systems. An example of a basic social class belief is our widespread acceptance of labels of social inferiority or social superiority about individuals and groups, as we try to adapt to the many varied communities and populations we inhabit.

When we use hierarchical principles in our thinking, and in our beliefs about social classes—such as dividing individuals and groups into superior and inferior categories—we necessarily apply our labels of social differences to this thinking. In so doing, we easily distort our identifications with the artificially constructed differences of social classes. This over-simplification of our complex social circumstances leads us to stereotype social realities, so that eventually we may believe in social class characteristics built on mistaken ideas. The relentless social processes activated by our beliefs in the importance or significance of superior and inferior categories, ultimately lead us to an unquestioning emotional acceptance of damaging or destructive stereotypes as social realities.

Our basic beliefs in hierarchies of individuals, groups, and social classes, compartmentalize our understanding of human differences, so that they are frequently accepted as social facts. This means that we do not question our individual and social distortions of social classes, thereby maintaining and perpetuating already established social classes. Even though our basic beliefs about social classes derive directly from our continuing experiences of social classes, we tend to maximize rather than minimize our traditional social class differences, because we have not reformed our thinking about social classes. Furthermore, social intelligence predicts that, as long as we depend on hierarchical principles to organize our thinking about other people, we inevitably perpetuate false hierarchical social class differences.

However, social intelligence also suggests that we need not define our individual and social experiences according to hierarchical social class beliefs. For example, when we value egalitarian—or more equal—relationships with others more than social classes, we necessarily modify our social class systems to some degree. Nevertheless, at present, even though we may have some social mobility within and between social classes based on material assets, gender, sexual orientation, race, or ethnicity, our freedom consists largely of moving up or down a social hierarchy in relation to these classes. Thus our beliefs about the necessity of social hierarchies still strongly limit our experiences of real social mobility. In fact, unless we truly embrace a wide variety of alternative human experiences and possibilities, we will be unable to effectively diminish the power of our existing social classes—and their related beliefs— in our personal and public lives.

In addition to believing in human categories or labels, such as being better or worse than others, another basic belief about social classes is our shared preferences to move toward—rather than away from—social classes associated with the greatest social privileges and rewards. Basic social class beliefs endorse the benefits of upward social mobility, rather than downward social mobility, so that we continuously deal with widespread restless strivings to achieve upper class statuses. At the same time, our constant yearning for upward mobility is inevitably accompanied by some rejection of our authentic experiences and real social circumstances. These basic beliefs in the advantages of upward social mobility therefore easily create widespread dissatisfaction and resentment, especially where there are insufficient opportunities for some individuals and groups to be upwardly socially mobile.

As long as we believe in the validity of superior and inferior social class categories, and the value of upward social mobility, we predispose our social relations and contributions to society toward maintaining the status quo. If, by contrast, we use our social intelligence to relinquish our largely unthinking emotional allegiances to social class hierarchies and social class mobility, we begin to open up our beliefs to wider ranges of values about human diversity and human achievements. This is not a utopian ideal, but rather a practical adjustment to reduce the destructive consequences of social classes in our current complex worlds. When we increase our social intelligence, as well as the social intelligence of others, we move more decisively toward minimizing social class biases and creating brighter futures.

Unique Social Class Beliefs

Our unique social class beliefs are directly related to our basic social class beliefs. They underlie the many specific ways in which we apply our basic social class beliefs to our everyday thinking and actions. We translate our basic social class beliefs into personally unique social class beliefs, for example, in order to more fully accept the fundamental hierarchy of our social classes in how we earn our livelihoods, how we dress, where we live, and how we relate to other people. Social intelligence helps us to be aware of the myriad ways in which social classes influence our day-to-day behavior, by recognizing that our actions flow from both our basic and our unique social class beliefs and assumptions.

When we accept the social hierarchies of our basic social class beliefs, we automatically buy into beliefs that unique social class distinctions apply to the whole of our lives. Making social class distinctions between genders, for example, means that we necessarily get caught up with the unique social class beliefs that apply to our own genders. Because male and female values often have fairly clearly marked contrasts, as well as hierarchical differences in power and statuses between males and females, unique social class beliefs and behaviors inevitably modify our gender activities, social relations, and community contributions. For example, women often strive to enter public arenas, in order to increase their social class statuses.

Unique social class beliefs also emerge from our basic social class beliefs in relation to financial categories. The quantity of material assets we have is often a significant aspect of our basic social class beliefs, whereas how we attain our assets, or how we spend our assets, frequently expresses our more subtly nuanced unique social class beliefs. Although our unique social class beliefs about finances—how we decide to live out our economic class differences—may not be as important as our basic social class beliefs, they are significant because they maintain and sustain our basic social class beliefs. For example, our unique social class beliefs are both pervasive and influential. Social intelligence helps us to see that the concerns we have about which schools our children attend or should attend, often result more from our unique social class beliefs than from our assessments of real educational benefits for our children.

Our varied unique social class beliefs often obscure the power that social classes have over us. Rather than see our preferences, regarding our children's schooling, in terms of our unique social class beliefs, we like to think that we are actually weighing the pros and cons of the quality of education that our children receive. When we deny our unique social class preoccupations in this way, however, we automatically succumb to our elemental needs to maintain our social class positions through education, or to improve our opportunities for social class mobility through education.

Our unique social class beliefs also frequently cloud other ways in which our decisions are influenced by our deep-seated needs to be upwardly mobile within and among the hierarchical social classes in our societies. Although selecting medical strategies for attaining high health standards may seem unrelated to our unique social class beliefs, for example, social intelligence shows us that our health resources and practices are largely an extension of our social class lifestyles, or our social class resources and aspirations. We often want to achieve good health, so that we can continue to strive for upward social mobility. We also sometimes refuse to get out of the rat races that characterize some highly competitive professions, because our unique social class beliefs encourage us to act in ways which improve our health, protect our social class statuses, and increase our chances for professional success or upward social mobility.

By showing us the extent to which we are dominated by our social class beliefs and pressures, that encourage us to stay in the game of maintaining our social class systems, social intelligence suggests ways to reduce the power of both our basic social class beliefs and our unique social class beliefs. For example, once we see the pervasiveness and power of our social class beliefs, we begin think more clearly about whether or not we really want to follow social class dictates. Furthermore, the sheer emotional overload of pressures, caused by the pervasiveness of our unique social class beliefs, may encourage us to use social intelligence to change the power that social classes wield over us.

Because it is not only the meanings of our unique social class beliefs, but also their qualities that affect their impacts, we need to consider some of the effects of having either rigid or flexible social class beliefs. This strategy is useful for assessing our options for changing our social class beliefs, as well as for creating ways to nurture social justice in relation to our social class beliefs. Developing alternative purposes and directions for our actions eventually reduces our unintended tendencies to perpetuate social class beliefs that reinforce unjust social class divisions.

Rigid Social Class Beliefs

Historically rigid social class beliefs had marked impacts on different populations and societies, increasing our human propensities to create and perpetuate rituals and traditions to meet our needs to survive. Rigid social class beliefs were the order of the day in past historic times, and because they were relatively clear-cut, it was correspondingly easy to pass them on from generation to generation. Rigid social class beliefs brought order and stability to societies, and assured populations that certain tasks would be accomplished to meet basic individual and social needs. For example, rigid social class beliefs ensured that sufficient numbers of members of the lowest social classes would be willing to undertake societies' most unpleasant necessary chores, so that societies could sustain their populations.

It was not until this artificial sense of orderliness in societies was shaken up by human discoveries and inventions—as well as by political strife, revolutions, and warfare—that our rigid social class beliefs were replaced by more flexible social class beliefs about the importance of increased opportunities, social justice, and a common good shared by all. Civilization progressed when alienation, which was at least in part brought about by rigid social class beliefs, was decreased by the acceptance of more open, more flexible social class beliefs throughout societies. This increase in open, flexible social class beliefs also made social justice more likely to be achieved.

Social intelligence requires that we reflect and learn from these past individual and social experiences, so that we can draw some valuable practical conclusions about the negative consequences of rigid social class beliefs. For example, we increase our social intelligence when we compare social class beliefs in varied historical contexts, because we understand more fully how rigid social class beliefs are unquestioningly more damaging to individuals, groups, and societies than flexible social class beliefs. It is a social fact that deterministic beliefs—rigid social class beliefs—suggest a universe which is essentially devoid of human choices, as well as a status quo that cannot be changed. To the extent that social classes are believed to be castes, with powerful religious or secular sanctions that keep generation after generation of family members in the same social classes, their resulting world views are necessarily limited regarding individuals' or societies' present and future options.

Ultimately rigid social class beliefs provide rationales about the impossibility of social mobility. Thus rigid social class beliefs essentially imprison individuals, communities, and societies in patterns of fatalistic, deterministic thinking and acting, which prolong and perpetuate problematic social class conditions. Continuing closures of opportunities increase the entrenchment of people's social class beliefs, so that repetitions in these negative and destructive beliefs and social conditions are difficult to break.

Social intelligence shows us how rigid social class beliefs work together with traditions and other social practices to bring about closed social class structures. The harm done by the substance of our social class beliefs, results from the fact that we act in accordance with these beliefs, even though they often do not reflect the most significant objective conditions in our lives. Furthermore, in spite of becoming aware of those objective social facts which affect us the most, we may easily spend our lives using social class beliefs based on outdated or false assumptions, which perpetually misguide us. In these respects, holding on to rigid social class beliefs that close off our opportunities for change, has particularly pernicious consequences. Social intelligence is a wake-up call to more realistically and more accurately assess our true living conditions, so that we begin to replace our destructive rigid social class beliefs with more constructive, flexible social class beliefs.

However, these improvements are not easily achieved. It is often extremely challenging to design socially intelligent strategies which predictably initiate effective changes in our rigid social class beliefs. This means that we may have to wait until crises arise—such as job losses—which destabilize our rigid social class beliefs, and allow us to make more objective reassessments of our options to change our restrictive social class beliefs. Because our rigid social class beliefs tend to be perpetuated, in spite of considerable evidence which contradicts their validity, it may be only when the foundations of our rigid social class beliefs are threatened, that more constructive changes occur.

Optimally our rigid social class beliefs need not only to be shattered in this way, but also to be replaced by more flexible social class beliefs. We cannot exist without harboring some beliefs, and the more constructive our social class beliefs are, the more productive our behavior will be. Because of the dominance of social classes in our everyday lives, whatever our social circumstances, it is imperative that we formulate some clear ideas about social classes, and how we want to conduct our lives in relation to social classes. Although our beliefs do not determine our realities, they predispose us to understand situations and act in specific ways, as well as to select particular opportunities for constructive or destructive purposes.

Flexible Social Class Beliefs

Cultivating meaningful and viable flexible social class beliefs is a successful way to avoid some of the negative consequences of living according to rigid social class beliefs. Given the enduring social origins of all our beliefs about social classes, our most socially intelligent option is to identify and develop flexible social class beliefs, which increase the openness of our social classes, rather than rigid social class beliefs, which perpetuate caste-like social class divisions.

Flexible social class beliefs include many different criteria according to which people stratify their relationships with each other, as well as many different ways to create opportunities for social class mobility, or to neutralize the negative impacts of existing social classes. Because most social classes are built on arbitrary social characteristics, using social intelligence to become more objective about existing social classes, helps us not to take established social class criteria too seriously. For example, we may laugh at ourselves in order to come to terms with our over-commitments to pursuing narrow social class goals in the past. When we develop fresh views of ourselves we see social classes differently, find opportunities for strategic actions, and neutralize the negative impacts of existing social classes.

Becoming more socially intelligent increases our freedom to choose more meaningful goals. We no longer toe the line for what we believed was social class acceptance, which consequently enables us to ask deeper questions about objectives that may represent downward social mobility, rather than the more conventionally aspired to goals for upward social mobility. When we find goals which increase purpose and direction in our everyday actions, social intelligence supports us in our recognition that one of our most significant privileges is to be free of the compelling dictates, fads, and fashions of traditional social class criteria.

Social intelligence increases our knowledge about the many complex ways in which societies influence our social class beliefs. When we understand social influences more astutely, we broaden our perspectives, increase our options, and make our beliefs more open and more flexible. Becoming more socially intelligent enables us to loosen the hold that social influences have on our well-being, so that we become more whole in our responses to our particular social situations. We no longer seek the security of social class memberships, for example, because we are better equipped to deal with social forces in our existential dilemmas, as well as to change how we make our choices. This gives us sufficient freedom to pursue more heartfelt, ethical goals, such as increasing social justice.

We neutralize the damaging consequences of having rigid social class beliefs about our goals, when we recognize their limited social origins, and compare them to the more complex social origins of flexible social class beliefs and their goals. Seeing the power and complexity of flexible social class beliefs more clearly, enables us to select goals that yield the most meaning, without succumbing to the arbitrary beliefs of social class hierarchies. Although this shift in our attention and energies is not easy to accomplish, and is inevitably accompanied by new trials and tribulations, these battles are worth fighting, because they ultimately increase our freedom and effectiveness, as well as others' freedom and effectiveness.

III. Social Classes

In the long run, flexible social class beliefs open up opportunities for more people, because they ensure that we see others in the same holistic ways that we see ourselves. We are in stronger positions to encourage our children, and members of our youngest generations, to gain sufficient courage to pursue meaningful social ideals, so that we can work together cooperatively to increase the common good and social justice.

To the extent that we are successful in creating a momentum to achieve these qualitative changes, we free ourselves from historical imperatives to perpetuate traditional social classes. When we loosen the hold that social class traditions have over us, for example, we invent new patterns of behavior, as well as create innovative social arrangements in societies. We design more meaningful futures, and find more benign and more effective ways to organize our needs to survive and be fulfilled.

Knowing the power of our social class beliefs, how they entrapped us in the past, and how they continue to limit our present and futures, predisposes us to change them. This is a complex process, and ideally we need to be able to assess others' social class beliefs, as well as to choose our own goals. This is so because it is our collective efforts—rather than our individual initiatives—that eventually increase social justice and the common good.

Changing Social Class Beliefs

Social intelligence makes developing constructive social class beliefs more possible and more likely. When we start our days' activities with a firm understanding of the importance of social classes in our lives, together with awareness about their tenacity and pervasiveness in all aspects of our social situations, we are markedly better equipped to act so that we reduce or neutralize the negative influences of traditional social class definitions and expectations. By contrast, without the enlightening perspectives of social intelligence, we automatically accept those beliefs, values, and patterns of interactions that uphold and sustain traditional social class beliefs.

One way to break through the hierarchical assumptions and priorities, of our own established social class beliefs, is to consider ourselves as members of humankind, as well as of particular social classes. When we appreciate more fully what some of the common denominators of the human condition are, we can ask important existential questions, such as why human nature is not honored more than the arbitrary characteristics that we have historically and habitually assigned to distinguish different social classes from each other. Also, we can focus on such issues as the extent to which increasing social justice helps us to develop an ethic of egalitarianism in populations, or why individuals live up to their potentials more fully if they are not labeled in harmful, distorted ways.

Social intelligence gives us these broad perspectives on social classes, as well as on the social conditions of human life. We increase our social intelligence at the same time that we deepen our understanding of how we identify with a variety of social classes, and how others place us in different social classes. We must also consider whether our beliefs about our own social classes outweigh the power of others' beliefs about our social classes, because our successes in changing our social class beliefs is limited by whose social class beliefs we allow to restrict us.

Social intelligence shows us that increasing our knowledge about what we consider to be our own social classes, as well as heightening our awareness of how others attribute particular social classes to us, makes our efforts to change our social class beliefs more effective. When we are more objective about the starting points of what our own and others' beliefs about our social classes are, we increase our possibilities of using reliable strategies to change our social class beliefs. When we know what our social class beliefs are, we find meaningful ways to start the hard work necessary to change our social class beliefs, especially those beliefs which limit our options and opportunities the most.

This challenging task is made easier by focusing on where we want to go with our social class beliefs, what we want to achieve, and how we choose to relate to others. In other words, as well as knowing where we are coming from, we need to clarify the directions in which we want to go. Because the breadth of vision of social intelligence facilitates finding constructive opportunities to achieve these goals, social intelligence is both enlightening and inspiring. We acquire the strength to get through difficult parts of our lives, such as assessing the restrictive limitations of our social class beliefs, when we are able to consider more ideal trajectories for our energies and contributions to the common good.

The processes of finding goals which transcend our preoccupations with social classes eventually link us to social justice issues. For example, when we are sufficiently confident in our abilities to be more idealistic in our actions, we are more likely to discover or create ways to reduce some of the pain and suffering that flow from social class injustices. Beginning to live as though tomorrow's improved society is already here today increases our energies, as well as helps us to find myriad ways to make meaningful contributions to the common good.

As we continue to move toward social justice, we become more convinced that even though all societies in all places and at all times have had similar hierarchical social class arrangements, destructive social classes are not inevitable. Furthermore, social intelligence suggests that we pioneer particular changes in social class beliefs and social classes, at the same time that we reduce or neutralize the most negative impacts of social classes.

Nurturing Social Justice

When we turn our attention away from changing social class beliefs to how to nurture or increase social justice—usually by making contributing to the common good a high priority in our day-to-day lives—we necessarily call into question some important aspects of our social class beliefs. However, because our associations of social class beliefs and social justice may not immediately be obvious, we may have to deliberately reflect and consider what social intelligence implies before these connections can be made.

It is only when we understand the pervasiveness and power of our social class beliefs, that we realize their impact on the values we hold about ourselves and others. For example, when we do not question the validity of our social class beliefs, members of upper social classes often find it difficult to imagine what lower social class restrictions are like. If we do not intentionally build our social intelligence, it may be virtually impossible to have empathy for those who do not enjoy our own social class privileges. Similarly, if we are members of lower social classes, it is difficult to appreciate that stresses derive from being privileged, or that devastating accidents can quickly decimate upper social class members' material privileges or prized relationships.

The development of deep and mature capacities to understand others, especially from the points of view of their social class privileges or disadvantages, is an important aspect of both social intelligence and social justice. We are not socially intelligent unless we recognize and appreciate our own privileges—whichever social class we belong to—as well as realize the relative lacks of opportunities of those who are less privileged than we are. Because our lives are so caught up in social class activities, we need to constantly remind ourselves that however hard we try to change our own social class beliefs, most people will continue to think about social class memberships in relatively traditional or conventional ways.

Nevertheless, in a future where sufficiently large numbers of people change their beliefs about social classes, so that more egalitarian or more open possibilities for all are embraced, the negative impacts of social class beliefs will be lessened or neutralized. By contrast, whenever our lives are more or less determined by our social class beliefs, our accomplishments are necessarily diminished. Although it is possible to change our own social class beliefs, as well as have constructive impacts on those who do not necessarily share our social class beliefs, the power of traditional social class beliefs and actions is overwhelming.

Given these perspectives and odds, can we still conclude that the tremendous effort involved in changing our social class beliefs makes it worth our while to do so? Fatalistic or deterministic negative responses to this question are grossly inadequate or inappropriate. By contrast, social intelligence allows us to see that even seemingly slight or insignificant changes in one person's social class beliefs can essentially transform that person's life, as well as inspire countless others to make similar changes. Striving to increase social justice, especially along lines of challenging established social class beliefs, is usually very worthwhile, even though the immediate benefits of these efforts may not easily be assessed.

Social class structures, beliefs, and expectations in modern societies also change in spite of themselves, so that links between social class beliefs and social justice are modified. For example, social justice in modern societies may be more related to social classes based on gender, sexual orientation, race, and ethnicity than ever before, and newer social class criteria—like ablebodiedness and health—are scrutinized carefully for the first time. Rights and obligations, with regard to our most recent social class criteria, often have yet to be considered, especially if modern societies are to have a viable common good and pervasive, meaningful social justice.

When social class beliefs change automatically through time, due to historical shifts in the importance of financial assets, education, or other more traditional social class criteria, social justice issues are also affected. However, to the extent that particular basic beliefs about social classes continue to be dominant, social justice must continue to assess the viability or value of hierarchical social orders and social mobility.

Even though it is highly likely that social classes will continue to be important in the future, social intelligence suggests that we should continue to identify unjust shared beliefs and values about social classes in modern societies. Complex, distinctive cultures and lifestyles underpin our modern social classes, and these cultures may challenge our understanding of social justice, as well as our capacities to change our social class beliefs.

IV. Cultures

Our beliefs also derive from our cultures—especially from those values and ideals which individuals, groups, and societies cherish the most. To a certain extent, our cultures are extensions of our social classes. Social class values and ideals essentially uphold the statuses of individuals and the legitimacy of stratification systems, as well as define mainstream society. For example, we learn how to be middle class by cherishing middle class values and ideals, and by aspiring to goals which make us identify more closely with our middle class status.

This does not mean, however, that our cultures are merely products of our social classes, or that our cultural beliefs are the same as our social class beliefs. In spite of many overlaps between social classes and cultures, cultures also have a degree of autonomy or independence, which adds distinctive significance to the cultural origins of our beliefs.

Some of these specific dimensions of our cultures are social roots or social conduits of our beliefs. Fairly clear-cut categories or contrasts in beliefs—like traditional or modern beliefs, religious or secular beliefs, and beliefs about facts or myths—cut across social class lines, and create moralistic, artistic, or scientific repertoires of cultural beliefs. For example, we express our learning, experiences, or tastes by articulating our cultural beliefs, and we assess where we stand in history by contrasting our traditional and modern beliefs.

In many respects we are what we believe, and we usually believe in many complex aspects and nuances of our cultural worlds. Large repositories of social beliefs—like knowledge and education—are powerful cultural influences, as well as laws, customs, and traditions. Furthermore, we are human because we succeed in internalizing particular cultural beliefs, and we aspire to increase social justice when we make specific cultural ideals our own.

We may choose to be intensely patriotic within our cultures. Such close sharing of national cultural beliefs helps to bond populations, especially in times of war or strife. However, tightly-knit, overlapping beliefs also polarize groups and nations, so we need to establish sufficient openness in our shared cultural beliefs, in order to achieve peaceful coexistence. If we are too zealous, or too ethnocentric, about our cultural beliefs, for example, they may become weapons or means of separation, which exclude those with whom we do not identify or do not want to identify.

Closed cultural beliefs also produce prejudice and discrimination. Unless we are deliberately inclusive in our cultural beliefs, with a deep acceptance of true diversity, we find that our exclusive beliefs polarize us in relation to other groups. Such polarization prevents or restricts unity, so that conflict is created and justified, rather than consensus or cooperation.

Technological discoveries in the twentieth and twenty-first centuries speeded up travel, and made travel more available to the masses. Consequently, we have more cultural exchanges than ever before. Emigration and immigration movements challenge some countries to encourage immigrants to accept their host cultures, but there is also considerable haphazard or reluctant tolerance of what may be stark contrasts in cultural beliefs. Urbanization and media communications make cultural contrasts within populations more obvious, with the result that they cannot easily be avoided. Social intelligence shows us that, in order make meaningful and effective adaptations to new cultures, we need to be somewhat flexible in our own cultural beliefs, either as residents of established communities, or as cultural newcomers.

As when examining the social sources of our other major, influential beliefs, we discover widespread basic cultural beliefs, which are shared to some extent by many populations, as well as more specialized beliefs, which are usually produced by unique groups within societies. We also find that we can hold on to our cultural beliefs firmly or rigidly, or we can hold on to them with flexibility and creativity. Other significant choices in relation to our cultural beliefs are that we can welcome cultural changes by becoming agents of cultural change; we can actively resist innovation; or we can be passive receptacles and carriers of culture. These cultural beliefs reflect the existential dilemmas we necessarily face and deal with, as we rebuild or build our communities, societies, and civilizations.

Given wide variations in the social sources of our cultural beliefs, as well as among the specific cultural beliefs that drive our everyday decisions and actions, social intelligence guides us to select those cultural beliefs that most directly reflect our own interests and social justice. Even though societies and cultures frequently produce cultural beliefs and values which are in conflict with each other, we can decide which cultural beliefs and which values to make our own. Because our cultural beliefs are strong influences on our actions, we must make responsible decisions in selecting and nurturing shared cultural beliefs, so that we can play significant parts in enabling disadvantaged groups to be independent, to pursue their own interests, and to be fulfilled.

Basic Cultural Beliefs

Basic cultural beliefs provide us with ideas and ideals to define ourselves, others, and our environment. For example, the words and ideas we use to explain our individual and social realities express those meanings and beliefs that we apply to our social situations, and they help us to assess who we are—or where we are—in relation to our communities and societies.

Our cultures and cultural beliefs provide us with vital meanings that help us to survive. We understand our circumstances more fully, for example, because we share cultural vocabularies and cultural contexts that provide substance and perspectives for beliefs which explain our situations. Seeing ourselves as actors in our own cultural and social arenas allows us to formulate meaningful and appropriate goals, objectives, and ideals. Furthermore, in order to visualize tomorrow's world, we need cultural tools and capacities that enlarge rather than diminish our imaginations, so that we can see what a better world would be like.

The media magnify the effects of the inescapable fact that cultural beliefs permeate our societies and our lives. Our basic, most widely shared cultural beliefs become increasingly visible because of the omnipresence of culture in modern societies. Even though nuances are expressed largely through our unique cultural beliefs, some aspects of our basic cultural beliefs seem to exist in most situations. Because we cannot avoid the impacts and consequences of our cultures, we risk becoming entrapped—to some extent—by our relatively unchanging basic cultural beliefs. For example, when we acknowledge that some cultural influences are beyond our direct control, we often depend on basic cultural beliefs to give us the security and inspiration we need to protect us, even though established ways of doing things may not be in our own best interests. However, dreams in the most personal and private aspects of our everyday lives are also permeated with some basic cultural beliefs, which reinforce both our conscious and unconscious cultural habits and behavior.

We take steps to change our basic cultural beliefs when our social intelligence shows us their inaccuracies or inadequacies. The new basic cultural beliefs we consequently adopt may transform our daily existence. For example, when we are more aware of how we use our basic cultural beliefs to understand the passage of time, we may decide to choose basic cultural beliefs which value the present more than the past or the future, so that our cultural orientations to our daily needs become markedly different from what they were previously.

Even though we may persist in using our new basic cultural beliefs, rather than our former basic cultural beliefs that outlived their usefulness, we may experience uncomfortable transitions while acclimating ourselves to our new cultural starting points and new cultural attitudes. These reactions are evidence of the fact that selecting new basic cultural beliefs often makes considerable differences in how we behave, because doing this essentially redefines ourselves and our goals.

Our civilizations are built on our cultural beliefs, and most especially on our basic cultural beliefs. Boundaries between neighboring countries are also upheld by our basic cultural beliefs, and our most influential attitudes about war and peace derive from our basic cultural beliefs. Thus our basic cultural beliefs often predispose us to act, or not to act, as well as to construct or destroy societies.

Social intelligence helps us to realize the pervasiveness of our cultural beliefs, as well as what our basic cultural beliefs are. Social intelligence also shows us which of our basic cultural beliefs are more constructive or more destructive. Even when we are aware that our basic cultural beliefs are outdated, we need to develop a sufficiently sound cultural understanding of ourselves and our worlds from our experiences and observations, before we discard them. When we increase our objectivity by becoming more socially intelligent, we necessarily become more astute in making judgments about which basic cultural beliefs serve us best. We experiment with our new basic cultural beliefs through trial and error applications, for example, which make it possible to get on with our lives in more meaningful ways.

As long as our basic cultural beliefs are essentially hidden from us, it is difficult or impossible to recognize them and put them in order. This means that we have to dig deeply to unearth what our most basic cultural beliefs are, if we are to become more socially intelligent—a task which requires considerable time and energy. Scrutinizing our basic cultural beliefs in these ways may be more likely, when an external event shakes the foundations of our beings and our families. Dramatic changes in our circumstances, for example, more or less force us to make assessments and decisions that we would not usually make.

Some basic cultural beliefs often create harmony and consensus more than schisms and conflicts. For example, we can strengthen our collective strategies to achieve an expanded common good when we refine and make known what our basic cultural beliefs are. Furthermore, in many respects, our hopes for the future depend on making sure that our basic cultural beliefs are viable, so that we can act effectively as individuals, whole communities, and whole societies.

Unique Cultural Beliefs

The substance of our cultural beliefs changes with the times, as well as increases in complexity. Even though it is difficult to interpret precisely what the trends in these changing cultural beliefs are, we can distinguish unique cultural beliefs from basic cultural beliefs.

For example, we often make distinctions among our local, national, and global cultural beliefs by focusing on our more unique local and national cultural beliefs. Our smaller scale, unique local and national cultural beliefs frequently contrast with our comprehensive, sometimes integrated global or basic cultural beliefs. Moreover, we are often more ethnocentric in our local and national cultural beliefs, due to the uniqueness and strength of these cultural beliefs. By contrast, our global cultural beliefs often derive from some of the common denominators among the basic cultural beliefs of different societies. Thus our global cultural beliefs are made up of more general, widely-shared, basic cultural beliefs, rather than the more specific, unique cultural beliefs of individual societies and their varied regions.

Our unique cultural beliefs, at national levels, are frequently influenced by patriotism or national religions. Unique national cultural beliefs often express the dominance of particular political parties, because they reflect characteristics of societies at specific points in time. As a result, unique cultural beliefs at national levels are ever-changing, and may be in tension with broad global cultural beliefs.

Local areas also produce their own unique cultural beliefs, as do families and groups of families within these regions. Even though there are many distinctive patterns and repetitions in our unique regional cultural beliefs, they are often deeply rooted in the cultures of local families. The family roots of unique local cultural beliefs provide families and communities with some stability, so they may resist changes—including changes that would be in their long term interests. Because family roots enable local cultural beliefs to preserve their own uniqueness, this uniqueness often becomes sufficiently strong to withstand the momentum of external changes, which otherwise would inevitably lead to greater degrees of uniformity and conformity with respect to both national and global cultural beliefs.

As individuals, and as families, we learn how to pass on our unique combinations of cultural beliefs, which ground our unique local cultural beliefs more deeply. Sometimes, however, social tensions move us toward becoming integral parts of national and global trends, so that the strength of our unique local cultural beliefs must be deliberately increased in order for them to survive. For example, because the uniqueness of our cultural beliefs is damaged easily, we may need to protect our unique cultural beliefs from being overtaken or subsumed by the strong universalizing tendencies of global cultural beliefs, which often produce artificial homogeneity, rather than deeply-rooted diversity.

Beliefs and Social Intelligence

Social intelligence helps us to appreciate the importance and complexity of our unique cultural beliefs. For example, we need unique cultural beliefs to increase the number of choices we have in selecting cultural beliefs and values to guide us. The richness of our unique local and national beliefs enables us to create lively and meaningful identities for ourselves, so that we can pursue more adventurous directions in our daily lives, such as social justice. When we take the time, and make the effort, to nurture our unique cultural beliefs, we protect ourselves and grow stronger within our unique cultures. Much of our humanness—particularly our empathy—derives from the uniqueness of our cultural beliefs, so we have vested interests in not being absorbed by the broad trends of global or basic cultural beliefs.

Even though some patterns in global cultural beliefs are difficult to identify, many of these beliefs originate in the global market economy. Because global political systems are not as well-organized, or as efficient, as our global economy, the material values of the global market economy strongly influence the substance of our global or basic cultural beliefs. Where global market forces do not appear to be particularly strong, as in less industrially developed societies, considerable conflict may erupt due to these societies' contrasting cultural beliefs. In the long run, however, even these cultural conflicts may be absorbed by the growing influences of global market cultures.

Our unique cultural beliefs tend to be either rigid or flexible, and may either precipitate or resist change. Social intelligence suggests that we need to know the consequences of holding particular unique cultural beliefs, so that we can inform our choices in selecting what we consider to be the most constructive unique cultural beliefs as our own. We gain assurance and control over our lives when we understand the complexity and outcomes of our unique cultural beliefs, because then we can choose appropriate cultural beliefs to motivate us to increase the common good and social justice.

Rigid Cultural Beliefs
History often highlights the accomplishments of leaders and innovators who held rigid cultural beliefs. In fact, their heroic accomplishments are thought to depend on the clarity or vision that their fixed cultural beliefs brought. By emphasizing the positive results of some leaders and innovators, however, some of the problems or negative consequences that their rigid cultural beliefs engendered were ignored.

One of the pernicious results of clinging on to rigid cultural beliefs is that the vision that rigid cultural beliefs bring may be unrealistic, and therefore cannot be depended on to guide actions in a wide variety of situations in the long run. For example, although rigid cultural beliefs may inspire leaders and their followers to take timely strategic actions, they may not sustain populations during shifting circumstances through time.

Another harmful consequence of the use of rigid cultural beliefs to guide behavior is that the content of these beliefs too easily becomes dogma or bigotry. Clinging zealously to rigid unproductive cultural beliefs, and applying them indiscriminately to multiple situations, brings problematic consequences for all concerned.

In the long run we need cultural beliefs that open up our attitudes, so that we consider new possibilities and fresh opportunities, rather than repeat established trends or rituals. Fixed cultural beliefs diminish vital innovations, and their rigidity will not sustain us during the pressured give and take of crises, or even in monotonous and mundane everyday transactions. Our cultural beliefs need to be flexible, not rigid, if we are to pursue our chosen goals effectively through time.

Social intelligence helps us to make more accurate assessments of the strengths and weaknesses of both our rigid and our flexible cultural beliefs, because they have compelling consequences for our futures. Whatever basic or unique cultural beliefs we hold, these beliefs necessarily reflect our past or current social and cultural realities. Because all our beliefs have social origins, we understand ourselves more fully when we acknowledge the social origins of our cultural beliefs for what they are, and make more informed decisions about which cultural beliefs we want to honor through our actions. Social intelligence helps us to define our situations more accurately, so that we can select our most inspiring and most useful cultural beliefs to guide us.

To a certain extent singling out which cultural beliefs we want to nurture and cherish helps us to deepen our commitments to them. However, once we have decided which cultural beliefs to make our own, we need to incorporate them into our lives. This may work well for us, by sustaining our efforts during difficult situations, or it may backfire, by giving us too much of a fixed focus in our day-to-day behavior.

When we become overly fixated on a few cultural beliefs, we run the risk of making them rigid by tuning out other choices and possibilities. A narrowed focus for our decision-making and actions easily becomes counter-productive in our overall efforts to increase our social intelligence, and to live according to principles of social justice. This happens because our inadequately selected cultural beliefs become rigid, and stay fixed in a past that no longer exists, which prevents us from making successful adaptations to ongoing social changes.

Rigid cultural beliefs, whether they are produced by recent selections of cultural beliefs, or by patterns of interaction that took place in a distant past, block our progress toward achieving current goals that we want to accomplish. Rigid cultural beliefs close our minds to past, present, and future aspects of sizing up our social situations, and at the same time limit our capacities to make necessary adaptations to rapid social changes. They restrict our inclinations and abilities to imagine better circumstances, or to pursue social justice, so that we become relatively unable to undertake commitments and tasks that increase the common good and social justice.

IV. Cultures

When we realize that we are trapped by the rigidity of our cultural beliefs, we find ways out of our predicaments by giving a high priority to developing more flexible cultural beliefs. However, we cannot simply erase the problematic rigidity and predictability of our unproductive cultural beliefs. Rather, we need to find viable flexible cultural beliefs to substitute for our rigid cultural beliefs, so that we can accomplish our preferred goals. Some of the ways to do this are described in the following subsection of this chapter of *Beliefs and Social Intelligence.*

Flexible Cultural Beliefs

One of the most useful and most creative goals, in applying social intelligence to our everyday lives, is to formulate a small number of flexible cultural beliefs which represent our principles and deepest understanding of our social being. These flexible cultural beliefs serve us well when we allow them to guide us in directions we choose. They help us to adjust to current social trends, and form foundations for successful adaptations to those social pressures and influences that affect us the most. Flexible cultural beliefs also prepare us for unknown futures, and increase our creativity in dealing with wide ranges of individual and social problems.

Given the reality that most of us want to grow up quickly when we are children and adolescents, we often readily absorb others' fairly rigid cultural beliefs. Therefore, we need to replace our original rigid cultural beliefs with flexible cultural beliefs, if we are to act meaningfully and effectively. When we recognize the benefits of opening up our original rigid cultural beliefs—in order to embrace more flexible cultural beliefs such as equality, inclusiveness, diversity, cooperation, and openness—we begin to let go of those rigid cultural beliefs that damage us and others the most. During these significant, but often complex and difficult processes of substituting flexible cultural beliefs for our original rigid cultural beliefs, our ethnocentrism, dogmatism, bigotry, authoritarianism, and zealousness are diminished sufficiently to allow broader, more inclusive beliefs to take hold of our imaginations and actions. Thus we eventually replace the damaging narrowness of our former prejudices with broader ideals and life strategies.

At the same time that the flexibility of our cultural beliefs replaces our tendencies to act with prejudice and discrimination, we expand our options and the viability of our cultural and social choices. We are increasingly able to see which social and cultural issues need attention, in order to increase social justice, and we are correspondingly more able to make realistic and dependable commitments to participate in collective movements for social change, as well as to manage our own behavior. Although increasing our flexible cultural beliefs may turn our lives upside down, when we are more thoughtful in dealing with ourselves and others, we eventually live more meaningfully, as well as make more valuable contributions to our communities.

Our cultures are seas of changing beliefs, values, and ideals. Societies need cultures to motivate and move their members to adapt to the changing times of history, and individuals need cultures to orient their daily lives. Our searches for the meanings of our existence begin and end in our cultures, whether or not we consider particular sources such as traditional wisdom literatures or recent technologies. For example, adolescence is a life cycle stage when young adults are fascinated with and dependent on their peer cultures. By contrast, people with disabilities are often detached from their cultural situations, thereby increasing their isolation from mainstream societies. In spite of ourselves, our life choices are closely tied to specific cultural parameters and cultural options, so that our existential mandates include having to make sane cultural choices if we are to survive or increase the common good.

Because education is a significant part of our cultures, we make our cultural beliefs more flexible by continuing to educate ourselves about cultures' individual and social significance. We may choose to examine the wisdom literature of a particular religion, for example, or experiment by applying different religious axioms or principles to our daily activities. When we continue to use specific cultural beliefs to meet a wide variety of our daily needs, these beliefs necessarily become more flexible. We also benefit from seeing things more objectively, as well as from acting in accordance with new cultural premises and assumptions. When our preferred flexible cultural beliefs replace our hardened and inefficient rigid beliefs, they serve us better in accomplishing our goals, and in achieving social justice in troubled times.

Flexible cultural beliefs predispose us to make changes in our lives, as well as to increase social justice. When we free ourselves from the grip of our rigid, unproductive beliefs, we do not become less principled than we were before. Rather, our flexible cultural beliefs yield different principles. For example, instead of disseminating our rigid cultural beliefs about particular futures to others in authoritarian ways, we more productively concentrate our energies on the substance of flexible cultural beliefs, which fosters more democratic values, such as independent thinking. Our social intelligence and our cultural beliefs help us to encourage others to find their own truths and missions amidst our complex changing cultures.

Changing Cultural Beliefs

History shows us that different eras are dominated by contrasting cultural ideals and belief systems. In some respects this suggests that our local, national, and global cultures are independent, so that for better or for worse we are born into cultures that are in large part legacies of past generations. As a result, we have only limited opportunities to transform traditional cultures of the past, through applying our own preferred cultural beliefs during our lifetimes. Realizing this dilemma makes us face the existential challenge of the restricted impacts we have on our cultures, as well as question how we should transmit at least our most important cultural beliefs in the present for the future.

Our earliest recorded histories are largely made up of reports of warfare and political strife, rather than descriptions of cultural well-being and adequate living conditions. When social conditions were noted more systematically in our historical records, for example during rapid economic changes in the industrial revolution, or during waves of immigration and urbanization, we understood more fully how shared community traditions broke down, because they could no longer maintain or sustain cultural unity. In these eras of cultural change, new cultural beliefs and values emerged, due to increased travel, and to the increased juxtaposition of people from contrasting cultures and contrasting social classes in our cities. As a result, multicultural societies developed—a worldwide trend that continues today.

Our cultural beliefs have been in flux for the last few hundred years in modern societies. We experience more cultural diversity today than ever before, which is likely to increase in the centuries to come. It is therefore imperative that we find constructive ways to deal with these inevitable and predictable cultural contrasts, so that we do not inadvertently drift, or jettison ourselves into constant conflicts and wars. Either a realistic peaceful co-existence, or a more idealistic positive embrace of multiculturalism, is a worth-while goal in our efforts to increase cultural beliefs which uphold the common good or social justice.

Although these vast cultural changes frequently increase our senses of the inevitability of our futures, there is still much that we can do—as individuals and groups—to bring about our preferred changes. For example, cultural beliefs that derive from new or little-used values can become significant influences in reorganizing local, national, or international priorities. Furthermore, our everyday lives can be more or less transformed by changing our cultural beliefs. Beyond improving our life-satisfaction, for example, cultural changes can usher in vital, more widespread acceptances of our social responsibilities, which ultimately increase the common good and social justice.

As well as the local, national, and global trends toward multiculturalism, we experience deep cultural divisions and polarities in contemporary societies. For example, there are widely shared tensions between our long-established cultural traditions and modern cultural values, or between our religious beliefs and secular beliefs. Although it appears that these tendencies, if not schisms, will continue in the foreseeable future, it is possible to respect more of these differences in cultural values than we do at present, so that prejudice and discrimination are minimized rather than maximized. When we embrace cultural diversity, for example, rather than see it as a problem to be solved, we recognize that our cultural beliefs benefit, and become stronger, because of the richness that results from defining and expressing our cultural differences.

In some respects sharp contrasts in cultural varieties may be dulled or merged, due to our widespread social imperatives to adapt to changing circumstances. Groups that pursue shared modes of spirituality, for example, often try to recognize religions' varied approaches to worship, prayer, meditation, and doing good works. Also, when religious holidays are observed publicly, people with different religious beliefs frequently celebrate specific religious festivals together. These more open practices deepen our experiences and understanding of contrasting cultural beliefs, and make us more inclined to get along with others amicably, rather than to fight them.

It is against this backdrop of vast cultural shifts that we use social intelligence to focus on what we can do to influence our cultures and societies during our lifetimes. When we examine our basic and unique cultural beliefs from broad perspectives, for example, we see the realities, possibilities, and limitations of impacting societal or global currents of cultural change. Rather than being discouraged by the sheer enormity of this task, we recall how one person's innovative contributions had marked impacts on the course of history, as well as on the behavior or cultural standards of entire populations.

Realizing that our cultures are social phenomena that often need to be changed is an important beginning in bringing about cultural changes. Deliberately cultivating selected cultural ideals, such as social justice, provides us with directions for our actions and work, so that our efforts can follow some of the already-established traditions to increase the common good, by improving living conditions for all. We can also pursue more innovative cultural goals through educating ourselves and others, for example, so that we are not alone in trying to bring about constructive cultural changes.

Social intelligence shows us how having flexible cultural beliefs makes our efforts more successful and more effective than having rigid cultural beliefs. We are assured that we are doing all we can do, when we pursue our preferred cultural changes in a spirit of inquiry, openness, and objectivity, rather than indulge in destructive bigotry or zealousness. Ultimately, how we go about introducing new cultural beliefs and priorities to others may be as socially significant as what our new cultural beliefs are.

Nurturing Social Justice

Civilizations, in both our national and global cultures, were frequently based on the wisdom literatures of moral or religious teachings which addressed social justice issues. Furthermore, some of the most ancient histories of humankind are traced through describing the different perspectives of moral treatises. These narrations are evidence that moral principles, ethical knowledge, or rules of how to conduct our lives, are integral aspects of how we survive, as well as of how we are fulfilled.

IV. Cultures

When we decide to orient our lives toward becoming more knowledgeable about social justice, especially with view to incorporating social justice in our ideals and everyday behavior, we essentially decide to join longstanding traditions of altruistic behavior, which save others as well as ourselves. When we become sufficiently objective, as we increase our social intelligence, we make freer decisions to contribute to social justice and a common good for all.

One of the most significant benefits of deliberately nurturing social justice, as individuals and as groups, is that this orientation requires us to pursue ideals and goals that replace our more selfish or more destructive ends. Working toward increasing social justice turns our lives around—as individuals or groups—so that we more or less automatically choose different cultural beliefs to orient our day-to-day behavior.

We do not need to accomplish any particular aspect of social justice, as we deepen our understanding of social justice, in order to gain advantageous effects on our behavior and lives. We need merely make a sufficiently deep-seated decision to aim our actions toward cultivating social justice, as much as we can, in as many different situations as possible. Orienting our behavior toward increasing social justice helps us to become more aware of social influences, more alert to varied opportunities to make changes, and more committed to serving others.

If we are not yet able to make some of these rather dramatic changes in our everyday behavior and commitments, we should continue to nurture social justice by considering our options, observations, and intentions about social justice. What does social justice mean? To what extent is living according to social justice an existential imperative, or a pragmatic strategy? How does increasing social justice benefit me, my family, my community, and my society?

One of our findings, when we meditate about social justice, or ponder the advantages and disadvantages of social justice, is that there are many different answers to these questions. We each define and understand social justice according to our own cultural beliefs, but we can also work effectively with those who define social justice differently. We participate in collective action relatively harmoniously when we honor the same ideals of social justice, even though we may have contrasting rationales, approaches, and strategies. Consequently, including social justice in our lives does not reduce our cultural beliefs to uniformity in substance or expectations, but rather invites us to join historical and contemporary traditions in taking action to make the world a better place for more people.

Nurturing social justice, as well as using social justice to inspire our actions, flows directly from increasing our social intelligence. When we sharpen our awareness of the social sources of our cultural beliefs, and consider which of our cultural beliefs are basic, unique, rigid, or flexible, we start to change those cultural beliefs that block us from accomplishing our preferred goals. In the processes of substituting our most cherished cultural beliefs for our more negative cultural beliefs—or for those which are not as rewarding—we open our lives to increasing the well-being of others as well as ourselves. This means that we are now in advantageous positions for cultivating cultural beliefs that most directly represent and achieve social justice.

Social intelligence helps us to interpret our social situations differently. For example, we make use of our setbacks to strengthen our intentions to increase social justice and social intelligence. In fact, one of the most practical and most idealistic outcomes of applying social intelligence is to persist in our efforts to bring increased social justice to ourselves and those in need. Pointing our cultural beliefs in these directions motivates us to make the world a better place, so that future generations are not as likely to waste their energies and resources in unproductive conflicts or wars.

V. Societies

Even though societies, including our modern global society, are often extremely broad contexts for understanding our beliefs, societal beliefs are powerful influences on how we conduct ourselves. All sizes of societies are important social sources of our beliefs, because the substance or power of particular societal beliefs frequently depends on factors other than societies' sizes. For example, because some societies are massively broad in scope, they are not necessarily any more or any less important with respect to the influences of their beliefs on their populations' well-being, opportunities, and life outcomes. Being socially intelligent requires that we understand the different impacts that societal beliefs have on our behavior, so that we can be effective in what we set out to accomplish.

One of the advantages of viewing our beliefs in the context of societies is that we see relationships among our family beliefs, religious or secular beliefs, social class beliefs, cultural beliefs, and societal beliefs more clearly and more accurately. Families are selective in how they absorb their religious or secular beliefs, social class beliefs, cultural beliefs, and societal beliefs, for example, and putting all of these beliefs in their broadest societal contexts helps us to assess their influences on each other and on ourselves.

Some societal beliefs may assume more importance for individuals and groups than family beliefs, religious or secular beliefs, social class beliefs, and cultural beliefs. Influential societal beliefs include beliefs about gender, race, ethnicity, time, success, and health. Although beliefs about gender, race, and ethnicity have already been considered in *Beliefs and Social Intelligence* as special cases of social class beliefs, they can also be thought of as social institutions—or as foundations of societies—in their own right, which may assume great salience and power over what we do. Time, success, and health, by contrast, are usually relatively independent social influences, which have both overt and covert effects on how individuals and groups formulate their beliefs and actions.

The qualities and focuses of societal beliefs about gender, race, ethnicity, time, success, and health in large part determine the impacts they have on individuals and populations. When these beliefs are held with marked fervor, for example, they make their strongest impressions on our behavior and on establishing our priorities. Societal beliefs in time, success, and health influence the extent to which we may neutralize or negate social class influences, as well as other societal beliefs.

In examining societies as social sources of our beliefs, we need to be watchful for invisible or idiosyncratic beliefs which we take for granted, but which also influence us a great deal, whether we realize it or not. These less explicit beliefs include environmental beliefs, philosophical beliefs, and beliefs about style, fashion, sports, the media, illness, or the medical profession. Although these societal beliefs may appear to be random and superficial, some individuals and groups cling to them when defining themselves and orienting their actions.

Like our other most significant social beliefs, societal beliefs may be basic, unique, rigid, or flexible. Social intelligence helps us to decide which societal beliefs we want to change, in the interests of ourselves and others. Social intelligence also shows us to what extent our chosen societal beliefs lead us toward social justice. Whatever particular combination of societal beliefs we hold, becoming more objective about whom we are and what we want to accomplish is necessary for increasing our social intelligence, and for becoming sufficiently free to pursue our own goals.

Because the range of possibilities for societal beliefs goes beyond these specific examples, individuals and groups need to become aware of which societal beliefs they have internalized, and which influence their behavior the most, in order to free themselves from some of the negative impacts of societal beliefs. It is sometimes relatively easy for individuals or groups to substitute more constructive societal beliefs for destructive societal beliefs, depending on the salience of the meanings we attribute to the original negative societal beliefs we already accepted.

One starting point in these tasks is to observe which societal beliefs seem to work for those people we admire the most. For example, which societal beliefs help effective leaders to keep up with the times, as well as to make accurate assessments of everyday social conditions? Also, how can we learn what is most compelling about societies' beliefs, so that we increase rather than decrease our social intelligence? And, to what extent can we read serious newspapers specifically to increase our awareness of the world, and who we are in the global community?

Basic Societal Beliefs

Histories record some changes in societal beliefs over long periods of time. For example, labels like "The Age of Reason" are used to represent societal beliefs which were dominant in particular decades or centuries. Many societies have also moved from honoring traditional basic beliefs, to incorporating mainly modern basic beliefs. In these respects societies have changed their world views from being defined largely by religious beliefs, to world views founded on secular beliefs. Social intelligence points out that these historical trends show us how basic societal beliefs reflect widespread shifts in social conditions, and that basic societal beliefs are not static.

Some of our more structured, more fundamental societal beliefs include clusters of assumptions, perspectives, and world views. Societies formulate fairly general strategic postures with regard to their own populations, other countries, and the world, in order to survive. For example, societies may consider themselves as being somewhere between the extremes of friendly or unfriendly, offensive or defensive, historical or timeless, and materialistic or spiritual. Similarly societies may define their own populations, other countries, and the world as being powerless or powerful, cooperative or competitive, democratic or autocratic, and productive or unproductive.

The basic beliefs which we attribute to societies have strong influences on their populations, frequently in ways that are not obvious. In fact, the surreptitious impacts of societal assumptions may be stronger than societal beliefs that are either more apparent or more explicit. We behave like modern Westerners more or less automatically, for example, without being particularly aware of our own biases and prejudices as modern Westerners.

When our basic societal beliefs are made up of what we take for granted, we make assumptions about the overall standards of living in our countries. Our basic societal beliefs also include our assumptions about general levels of education, minimum wages, consumer patterns, housing, and lifestyles. Although a country's population may not have uniform, or even similar, experiences in these aspects of our everyday life, societies often have informal shared understandings about their circumstances, which are articulated as basic societal beliefs, such as "the American way of life."

We usually become most aware of the power our basic societal beliefs have when our countries are in social turmoil, in conflict with others, or at war. Whenever what we take for granted—such as our national security or peace—is threatened, we more easily imagine what our lives would be like without these conditions, which we depend on for our survival, productivity, and fulfillment.

V. Societies

Other basic societal beliefs, which are customarily evoked in uncertain historical times, concern important social or political issues such as resorting to arms and munitions, using prayer for societal support, or following the dictates of political leaders to resolve political conflicts. Even though we may want to participate in, or at least understand, our countries' policies during serious political crises, the strategic decision-making involved in resolving such strife is usually beyond the reach and comprehension of most people. Consequently, the basic societal beliefs called forth, in periods of marked social or political unrest, are often accompanied by widespread feelings of powerlessness. We then try to neutralize these difficult situations as much as possible by telling ourselves that we believe in, or trust, our political leaders and their social policies.

At best our basic societal beliefs stabilize us in political conflicts and wars. The social conditions that influence the well-being of our societies, as well as our individual and collective efforts to maintain the status quo, are supported by our basic societal beliefs about the nature of our societies, and our world views about viable relationships with other countries. Thus the primary purpose of many of our basic societal beliefs is to ensure our personal and collective security.

Our basic societal beliefs may be among our most deep-seated beliefs. This means that our basic societal beliefs are often extremely difficult to change, largely because we take them for granted, and because we need to be effectively integrated with our societies in order to survive. Social intelligence helps us to become aware of what our basic societal beliefs are, so that we can decide whether or not to continue to live with these beliefs. Our increased objectivity frees us to change our basic societal beliefs where needed, as well as our other social beliefs. Where changing our more destructive or more negative societal beliefs is too difficult to accomplish, our most viable solutions may be to leave our countries and live elsewhere.

Unique Societal Beliefs

Although basic societal beliefs are often shared among members of societies with similar geographical and economic conditions, unique societal beliefs are much less widely distributed, being characteristic of single societies rather than several societies. Our unique societal beliefs are more insular than our basic social beliefs, in that they reflect parochial or particularistic values rather than universal values.

Our unique societal beliefs can be defined as deriving from what makes societies distinctive. For example, our unique societal beliefs often create what we publicly recognize as the essence of our patriotism. This means that our unique societal beliefs are frequently called upon to increase the national unity of our populations and countries when needed, especially if political crises threaten individual and national security.

In times of both peace and war, our unique societal beliefs are integral parts of the particular histories and mythologies of our nation states. Our unique societal beliefs have capacities to quickly call forth the shared identity of a country, and they are essential dimensions of stories about the creation or development of that nation. Merely being members of the population of a society suggests that we share our unique societal beliefs to some extent, so that rejecting them may be viewed as tantamount to denying our biological, cultural, or political heritages.

We usually modify our unique societal beliefs dramatically after our childhoods only if we decide to become citizens of other countries. Decisions to leave our homelands are loaded with expectations and assumptions that adopting the unique societal beliefs of another country is necessary to function there as a citizen. In these situations, our adopted country's unique societal beliefs often become more significant than our homeland's unique societal beliefs, even though our original unique societal beliefs still necessarily influence our future decisions and behavior to some extent.

V. Societies

Social intelligence helps us to sort out which of our unique societal beliefs mean the most to us. These are the unique societal beliefs that we should keep and nurture, in order to improve the meaningfulness and effectiveness of our social actions. Becoming more objective about our unique societal beliefs helps us to respect their importance and significance, as well as to make those unique societal beliefs that support our other beliefs and actions our own.

Because our unique societal beliefs are not as widely shared with other people as our basic societal beliefs, it is often easier for us to change our unique societal beliefs than our basic societal beliefs. Social intelligence broadens our horizons, which loosens the tenacity of the grip of our unique societal beliefs. Although we still need to maintain our individuality, we understand more fully that holding on to particular clusters of unique societal beliefs may diminish our possibilities for actions, rather than create or maintain openness in our opportunities. Social intelligence shows us that we need to increase the flexibility of our most deep-seated connections to our local and national roots, so that we can go into the world to do whatever we have to do, rather than stay tightly bonded to relatively parochial traditional values of the past.

Because our unique societal beliefs frequently originate in national histories, or in the cultural values of specific political ascendancies, they may be more backward looking than our basic societal beliefs. The distinctiveness of our unique societal beliefs often develops from the rise and fall of those in power, so that their ideals derive from the past rather than orient us to the future. This means that over all, our unique societal beliefs may not be as productive or as creative resources as our basic societal beliefs.

Whatever hazards exist in making sound practical use of our unique societal beliefs, social intelligence helps us to make more effective decisions to protect ourselves, as well as to address issues that meet others' needs. Ideally, our interests in increasing social justice encourage us to be boldly selective in choosing our unique societal beliefs, so that we retain only those societal beliefs that expressly strengthen our identities, and enlighten our actions. Consequently, the scope and substance of our unique societal beliefs become realistic, dependable perspectives to be used in working on who we are, and what we want to accomplish.

Rigid Societal Beliefs

Rigid societal beliefs come in many shapes and sizes. Our histories show us that particular kinds of rigidity and closure in thinking about societies are potentially damaging to individual and social well-being. Therefore, social intelligence suggests that we should be wary of the lack of objectivity in, for example, ethnocentrism or religious fanaticism. Looking at such extremes of rigid societal beliefs helps us to understand the serious negative consequences of encouraging or entertaining rigid societal beliefs.

Ethnocentrism—the societal belief that one's own society is the central, most significant society in the world, as well as the best possible society—is often directly responsible for the development of a wide variety of rigid societal beliefs. When we have such an extreme bias in our societal perspectives, we cling to these beliefs, in order to make sure that they survive, at least to meet our own needs. On the other hand, if ethnocentric rigid societal beliefs are not widely shared, they do not endure through time. Their intrinsic unreliability, due to their closure to facts, often prompts many doubts, even though temporarily they may be experienced as vital and compelling societal beliefs in their own right. For example, when we are strongly ethnocentric in our world views, these rigid societal beliefs dominate our thoughts and permeate whatever we do.

The taken-for-granted assumptions, and closed belief systems, of ethnocentric rigid societal beliefs control our postures to self, other people, the world, and life. When we think we are morally right in our definitions of complex social realities, we close our eyes and ears to others' ideas and experiences, and we develop attitudes that foster prejudice and discrimination. Consequently, these rigid societal views and behavior become harmful to others. Furthermore, even though history shows us that atrocities like genocide result from nurturing ethnocentric rigid societal beliefs, we may not necessarily connect our own ethnocentrism with increasing possibilities for dangerously destructive behavior.

Genocide is the most serious, most world threatening outcome of ethnocentric rigid societal beliefs. Other destructive results of rigid societal beliefs pale by comparison, but nevertheless remain very significant, because they frequently lead to varied forms of extremism and fundamentalism. Given these facts, we need to find effective ways to call a halt to the early stages of these cumulative harmful processes, whether or not their lethal results seem imminent. The destructive outcomes of ethnocentric rigid societal beliefs are particularly important social issues, because they are life-threatening for the masses as well as for individuals.

One danger signal, which often becomes a precondition of ethnocentrism, is the development of rigid religious beliefs, especially those that spell out negative sanctions for nonbelievers. Although most religions suggest specific world views, religions that also emphasize harmful consequences for nonbelievers give rise to dangerous rigid societal beliefs. For example, historically, wars have been justified by religions that served as rigid and powerful social or political tools. The more zealous religious individuals or groups become, the more likely they are to increase the number of their potentially destructive rigid religious beliefs and practices. For example, people who have dogmatic religious beliefs are more likely to want to purify the world by dealing antagonistically and aggressively with nonbelievers.

Social intelligence helps us to assess the broad views and social implications of our rigid societal beliefs. Collecting information and increasing our objectivity about our social situations allow us to be more enlightened in our judgments, so that we can weigh the pros and cons of particular rigid societal beliefs more rationally. Social intelligence also enables us to be more honest with ourselves, so that we can avoid buying into rationalizations which perpetuate rigid societal beliefs, including those which are taken for granted, as well as those which are more explicit.

We use social intelligence to understand what our rigid societal beliefs are, so that we can make thoughtful substitutions in our societal beliefs which reduce, minimize, or eradicate their negative impacts. Only when we know what we believe, as well as what we want to achieve, are we in sufficiently advantageous positions to make these changes. Social intelligence shows us that it is usually injurious to hold on to our rigid societal beliefs, because they do not have sufficient productive or constructive consequences.

Social intelligence identifies our most harmful, rigid societal beliefs, as well as suggests replacements with life-enhancing beliefs. Thus social intelligence moves us toward social justice, even in spite of ourselves, by reducing our tendencies to perpetuate our rigid societal beliefs, and by reducing prejudice and discrimination in society. We not only become more selective about our societal beliefs through using social intelligence, but also more eager to increase social justice and the common good.

Flexible Societal Beliefs

Flexible societal beliefs do not have the same content as rigid societal beliefs. In fact, one of the main characteristics of flexible societal beliefs is their relative emptiness of clearly-defined ready-made meanings. The most important, central, flexible societal belief is that we need to remain socially aware in all circumstances, so that we can respond more effectively to ongoing social changes. Our flexible societal beliefs help us to maintain states of readiness, so that we can take actions—or not take actions—as high priorities.

In order to live fully in a particular society, we need to have a minimal number of basic societal beliefs that we share with other members of its population. Ideally, we should not clutter our minds and beings by nurturing contradictory societal beliefs, because societal beliefs which do not support our choices or actions directly are superfluous and cumbersome.

If we are to be socially intelligent, one of our main missions is to remain open to seeing, understanding, and absorbing new societal beliefs and new societal priorities, which enable us to move closer to what we want to accomplish. However, we need to remember that when we add new societal beliefs, in our quests to increase our social intelligence, we risk absorbing some nonproductive or contradictory beliefs, which ultimately block opportunities to achieve our goals.

We need to discriminate in selecting our societal beliefs, so that above all we remain flexible. Choosing to harbor or maintain unnecessary societal beliefs is inevitably counterproductive to our goals to improve the effectiveness of our actions through increasing our social intelligence. Even though our chosen societal beliefs are powerful influences on our personal behavior and collective actions, we also need to enhance our capacities to respond spontaneously, with awareness, to the complexities of our given or changing social situations.

Flexible societal beliefs provide sufficient space for us to grow, as well as increase our options for accomplishing individual and collective changes. They allow us to deal with our changing circumstances thoughtfully, as we grow and make changes. Given these priorities, flexible societal beliefs strengthen—rather than weaken—our capacities to reach our goals. The openness of our flexible societal beliefs ensures that we perpetuate our basic societal beliefs, and at the same time give us sufficient freedom to create new selves and new worlds.

Beliefs and Social Intelligence

Historical data show that it is not repeating traditions or patterns of the past that brings about increased opportunities for all, but rather new visions of futures and different ways of meeting basic societal needs. Whether individuals or groups create variations in how necessary tasks are accomplished, constructive social changes are related to the widespread acceptance of new emphases and new priorities in our societal beliefs. When we see and understand our resources differently, for example, we can initiate major social changes effectively, such as the industrial revolution.

Societal beliefs are sufficiently broad that they increase our historical awareness of who we are and what our current opportunities for change are. Cultivating flexible societal beliefs ensures that we move in constructive rather than destructive directions. Our options for societal beliefs need to be open, for example, in order to increase the purposefulness of our actions. By contrast, when we succumb to historical forces beyond our control, we cannot define our own destinies. We become relatively passive pawns in the creation of our futures, by automatically conforming to more traditional societal beliefs.

Changing our societal beliefs, staying open to new possibilities, and deliberately cultivating societal beliefs that are integrated with social justice ideals, enable us to be more in charge of our options and views of social possibilities. When we use our social intelligence to decide whether to accept or reject particular societal beliefs, we heighten our awareness of our options and priorities, so that we negotiate more effectively about our individual and collective preferences.

Leading lives which are relatively uncluttered by unnecessary societal beliefs gives us clarity and freedom. Our chosen flexible societal beliefs serve us well in dealing with the hurdles we need to surmount in order to accomplish our more enlightened goals. Our motivations to act increase, and we become more dedicated to social justice, as well as more open to possibilities for a new world.

V. Societies

Changing Societal Beliefs

History shows us that before systematic social records were kept, there was very little awareness about the circumstances, conditions, and organization of societies beyond local communities. In these early stages of civilization, the dearth of reliable communications made it impossible for most people to assess what was going on in whole societies. Consequently, societal beliefs were not as clearly formulated as they are today, and were difficult to change, due to people's low levels of broad social awareness. Inadequate communications and life-threatening means of transportation resulted in highly insular shared perspectives on society, which were often rooted in religious beliefs rather than facts.

Possibilities for articulating and changing our societal beliefs increased through time. However, it is only in relatively recent eras that populations have had sufficient information about their societies, and the world outside their boundaries, to be able to create realistic societal perspectives and beliefs. For the greater part of human evolution, human beings depended on severely limited views of society, together with a relatively diminished, short term understanding of human nature.

Increased travel, together with ongoing discoveries of territories and civilizations, awakened us to additional complexities and facts of human diversity. For example, we became more aware of the parochial nature of our contemporary world views, as well as those described in our historical records. Human naivety and ignorance had led to the development of beliefs about communities, rather than societies, which frequently evoked raw antagonisms rather than collective actions to establish broad social ideals such as social justice.

Our ideas about social justice are influenced by all our social beliefs, but sometimes especially by our societal beliefs. Only when we realize that we choose how to organize and conduct ourselves as societies, can we design effective strategies and make sufficiently deep commitments to achieve social justice. Thus our views of human possibilities are integrally related to how we select our societal beliefs, and how we act in societal contexts.

Social intelligence requires that we persist in our efforts to change our social beliefs about our families, religions, social classes, cultures, and societies. Sometimes we are not aware of what these beliefs are, where they come from, or how we can change them effectively. However, the more aware we become, the more likely we are to select and maintain those social beliefs that mean the most to us, including beliefs based on principles related to social justice.

Even though most of our social beliefs derive from our families, religions, social classes, cultures, or societies, it is our beliefs about societies that provide many of our broadest perspectives on our situations. Furthermore, and in some vital respects, it is generally easier for us to be objective, and to make changes in who we are, or in what we want to do, when we see ourselves in these broadest societal contexts. For example, when we are more emotionally distant from ourselves in the perspectives of our societal beliefs, we increase our objectivity and freedom to make changes. By contrast, when we examine social beliefs which emerge directly from our families, religions, social classes, and cultures, we may discover that we are so caught up with these more personal aspects of our lives, that it is extremely difficult to understand or change them.

Sometimes examining and changing our societal beliefs is intellectual rather than experiential. We begin to substitute societal beliefs we want to keep, for societal beliefs we do not want to have, when we recognize how each of our societal beliefs influences our decisions and actions. Seeing some of the limiting aspects of our societal beliefs may be sufficient motivation to accomplish such changes, especially when we continue to learn as much as we can about different societies. Furthermore, educating ourselves into new societal beliefs is frequently easier to accomplish than changing our beliefs about our families, religions, social classes, and cultures.

This fact, that it is often easier to change our societal beliefs than our other social beliefs, does not necessarily mean that changing our societal beliefs is either more or less important than changing our family, religious, social class, or cultural beliefs. Having an accurate or inspiring view of the world is a strong motivator for our behavior, and time and again we return to the larger picture of our lives for inspiration, especially when we live and work under duress. For example, we refresh ourselves when we pause to reflect by putting our lives in broad perspectives. Nevertheless, however universal our frames of reference are, as in our religious beliefs, we still need to size up who we are and where we want to go in our real worlds of social facts, especially if we choose to take meaningful actions to increase social justice.

Nurturing Social Justice

When we understand the influences that our societal beliefs have on our decisions and behavior, we are also more likely to make lasting commitments to nurture social justice. Because we do not become aware of social justice in a short period of time, and because we need constant reminders of its importance in our lives, we have to continue to re-educate ourselves about social justice, and how we can accomplish it on a daily basis. The knowledge base of social intelligence makes our contributions to the common good, and to social justice, more reliable and more meaningful.

Social intelligence guides us as we come to terms with our different situations and different beliefs. Connecting our particular beliefs to their social origins allows us to more fully appreciate the ways in which social conditions influence our destinies. However, unless we clarify our goals and objectives, we might not consider social justice as a viable option or direction for our efforts. When we deliberately express our interests in social justice, by allowing our beliefs in the importance of social justice to take root in our minds and in our behavior, social justice becomes a moving force in our lives.

The main questions to consider here are why social justice is important, and why we benefit from including social justice as a goal in our daily behavior. Social intelligence shows us that social conditions make considerable differences in our life outcomes, and that our own well-being ultimately depends on the well-being of others. When there is widespread alienation, unrest, conflict, and dissatisfaction in our societies, we are not in positions of strength, and the structures of these societies are threatened. Understanding individuals' necessary dependence on others encourages us to open up opportunities in our societies, so that increasing numbers of people can benefit from privileges that are usually enjoyed only by a few.

Therefore, perhaps we need to turn to social justice issues as pragmatists, if not for other reasons. Building strong, cooperative societies for the next generations is a worthwhile goal to pursue, and developing social justice will meet or advance such social ideals. Nurturing social justice eventually brings about direct results, like increasing equality in opportunities, as well as more idealistic consequences, like realizing that we are responsible for social changes, even when our goals are not aimed for expressly to increase social justice. All in all, however, nurturing and supporting social justice effectively guarantees the increased well-being of greater numbers of people and societies.

The practical goal of increasing social justice is achieved best by using our socially intelligent beliefs as dependable guides. For example, when we understand which of our societal beliefs influence us the most, we can assess them in light of our intentions to increase social justice, and at the same time discard those societal beliefs that do not motivate us to take action to increase social justice, or help us to actualize social justice goals.

V. Societies

Once we have assessed our beliefs about our families, religions, social classes, cultures, and societies, we are in advantageous positions to decide how we want our social beliefs to influence us. Selecting societal beliefs that mean the most to us frequently moves us toward some social justice ideals. Furthermore, pondering how we can nurture social justice encourages us to translate our daily challenges into actions, which both increase our social intelligence and increase social justice.

Although it is difficult to know when these idealistic goals are met, we can assess changes in our lives, especially those which suggest that what we do now is more significant than what we did in the past. We take stock of the clues and signs that suggest we are progressing toward social justice, through the changed social facts in our lives, and through others' responses to our views and actions. In the long term, we gain the satisfaction of knowing that our lives have both deepened purposes and more specific directions.

We do whatever we can to deal responsibly with our own situations, and then we turn to our communities and societies to build and serve the common good. These are the beliefs and inspiration that drive us forward as we increase our social intelligence, and our ultimate mission is creating a better world, rather than merely increasing our social intelligence. However, our social intelligence also reminds us that social issues are best addressed by taking collective actions to increase social justice.

Social Intelligence and Beliefs

VI. Taking Charge of Beliefs

Social intelligence brings new perspectives and new priorities
to our daily lives. We see things differently when we are
aware of the many ways in which social influences affect our
decisions and actions. Social intelligence also helps us to be
realistic and practical in assuming responsibilities for changing
how we act, especially when we try to improve our lives and
societies according to principles of social justice.

More specifically, social intelligence is the capacity to
control our decision-making and behavior in accordance with a
deep understanding of the complexity and power of social
influences. Those social influences that usually have the
strongest effects on us are our families, beliefs, social classes,
cultures, and societies. As we become adults, and more
emotionally mature, we regulate our active participation in these
social processes more thoughtfully. For example, we increase
our social intelligence, and become more effective historical
actors, to the extent that we take charge of our beliefs.

Once we understand how much social influences affect our life
outcomes, we find reasons to become socially intelligent, as well
as learn skills to maintain higher levels of social intelligence. It is
only by making choices about which beliefs we want to keep as
our own, however, that we take charge of our beliefs. As long as
we continue to incorporate others' beliefs into our lives, or try to
live according to others' expectations and standards, we lose touch
with who we are and what we want to do with our lives.

97

Social intelligence helps us to be ourselves, and helps us to act according to our own interests. Being socially intelligent means that we necessarily discard vicarious ways of believing and living when we fine-tune our connections with ourselves, and when we substitute our own carefully considered beliefs for others' beliefs. We take charge of our beliefs when we dare to be ourselves, deliberately selecting only those beliefs that are truly ours.

Social intelligence guides us in assessing the significance of our social actions, and shows us how to coordinate our beliefs and actions more effectively. This is possible because our social intelligence derives from a sound observed and experiential knowledge of the power and complexity of the major social influences of families, beliefs, social classes, cultures, and societies. We increase our social intelligence by increasing our knowledge about the impacts that our families, beliefs, social classes, cultures, and societies have on us, and on our definitions of our social situations.

Our capacities to understand constructive and destructive social influences increase as we become more aware of our social intelligence, and use it to guide our actions. Our understanding encourages us to make more responsible choices of beliefs, so that we are no longer as vulnerable to the whims and fancies of others. We learn how to stand our ground, for example, as well as how to deal with others' pressures, when we see more clearly what is really going on.

The broad and holistic perspectives of social intelligence also allow us to make direct connections between the past, present, and future. When we identify patterns in social influences which affect our past, present, and future, we find ways to loosen the grip of these impacts, so that we free ourselves from their most destructive negative consequences. In these ways social intelligence gives us breathing spaces in our daily routines, so that we can see and take action in relation to the broader and deeper gestalts of our connections to other people.

VI. Taking Charge of Beliefs

To a large extent our beliefs reflect our sacred and secular values, and plug us into the values of our families, social classes, cultures, and societies. Sometimes particular belief systems, such as religions or sciences, have clusters of beliefs, which imply specific groups of values. Furthermore, when we change our beliefs, we necessarily change our values, because of the close inter-relationships between our beliefs and our values.

Taking charge of our beliefs enables us to manage them more successfully in wide ranges of social situations. Social intelligence increases our awareness of the complex social origins and social consequences of our beliefs, as well as guides us to manage our beliefs. Ideally we try to understand whatever beliefs we have, before we decide to change them, with the realization that our resistance to letting go of our unproductive beliefs ultimately holds us back, and impedes our progress in becoming more socially intelligent.

We must consider and respect others, as well as ourselves, in the challenging processes of taking charge of our beliefs. Social intelligence helps us to focus on the tasks in hand, and guides us in the fact-gathering that makes changing our beliefs more meaningful and more worthwhile. For example, when we develop clearer identities as historical actors by making more responsible choices in our beliefs, we contribute more effectively to communities and societies in the present and future. Social intelligence helps us to select beliefs that we truly need, or that we consider to be most meaningful. Thus social intelligence becomes one of our most crucial capacities to choose wisely, which allows us to undertake more responsible and more effective actions to increase social justice.

Becoming an Historical Actor

In our earliest histories, historical actors were recorded as privileged individuals, such as kings or knights, rather than members of a country's rank and file population. In these

99

circumstances, historical consciousness was thought of as the culmination of years of education, or as the end point of social advantages gained from years of leisurely pursuits. Because there was very little democratization of social opportunities in early historical eras, privilege and social honor were narrowly defined, reflecting elitist lifestyles.

In today's societies, more people are directly involved with creating historical changes, through peaceful means as well as political strategies. As a result, we can now ponder what it takes—beyond social class privileges—to have significant historical impacts on our everyday social realities. What kind of individual and social consciousness do historical actors have? Are these attributes the same or different from social intelligence? What social responsibilities do we have as historical actors?

We answer these questions when we examine how people become historical actors, and how social intelligence prepares us to become effective historical actors. We need to understand which perspectives on our daily lives allow us to be historical actors, and how our beliefs influence our assessments of the social purposes of historical actors, or of societies' needs for historical actors.

We become historical actors when we see ourselves, our lives, other people, and our societies from both local and global perspectives, and act accordingly. Although these historical views of social realities are not as broad in scope as the perspectives of infinity that characterize religions, they provide us with meaningful opportunities to see the whole pictures of our lives.

Social intelligence encourages us to seek out, and make use of, these broad views of ourselves. Articulating the social sources and social contexts of our families, beliefs, social classes, cultures, and societies makes us more aware of the social underpinnings of historical changes, and the ways in which we are all necessarily historical actors, whether we act

100

deliberately as such or not. We cannot avoid the restrictions that historical time brings to our lives, and we understand ourselves and our possibilities better when we persist in considering the power of historical timing, and the broadest social contexts of our daily events.

Social intelligence changes our understanding and attitudes, as well as our assessments of social realities, so that we pursue more deliberately selected goals in our personal and public lives. We assess what we think we should be doing by summing up facts of our social situations, for example, and by working toward carefully chosen goals. At best being historical actors requires consistency in our actions, so that we eventually believe that we will achieve the goals we set ourselves. These beliefs motivate us to act, and we create or reinforce our new beliefs when we act.

Being historical actors requires that we increase our social intelligence by getting to know our families' histories, which necessarily fit into our national and international histories. Being historical actors also requires that we have sufficient social intelligence to understand the social origins and social scope of our beliefs, as well as the relationships between our beliefs and major social influences. Historical actors use social intelligence to understand linkages between our social classes and cultures, and to consider our national and global societies as the broadest arenas of our actions. When we move freely between these different perspectives, or levels of thinking, we are more likely to become historical actors through coordinating our behavior, goals, and social initiatives.

An historical actor has purpose and direction, which is expressed most directly through addressing and responding to specific goals. Historical actors pay attention to major social influences, in order to pursue well-considered objectives effectively, and to respond to populations' real needs. These intentions and actions include increasing social justice, and they ensure that we continue to increase our social intelligence as we work toward increasing the common good. Historical actors often dedicate themselves to serving others, which we accomplish best when our own needs and those of our families have already been met.

We attain and maintain objectivity by standing outside our personal lives, so that we more easily distinguish between the real and unreal needs of others, as well as more carefully harvest and make good use of our energies. Our efficiency and productivity depend in large part on the level of our social intelligence—we work most effectively toward increasing the common good, as historical actors, when we understand the power and complexities of social influences.

Responsible Choices

History shows us that responsibilities vary widely, depending on the demands or needs in particular historical or social conditions. Definitions of responsibilities also vary according to gender, race, or ethnicity. However, there are some common denominators among different kinds of responsibilities, or shared aspects of the more universal characteristics of responsibilities. These generally include being knowledgeable, in advance, about the most probable outcomes of our individual and social actions, as well as acting in ways which are constructive rather than destructive in their social consequences.

Social intelligence helps us to take charge of our beliefs, which means that we can then make more responsible choices. When we become historical actors, by maintaining broader and deeper contexts for understanding our actions and social conditions, we necessarily continue to make more responsible choices through time, as well as in different sets of circumstances.

When we use social intelligence to guide us in collecting social facts, we become relatively well-informed about the likelihood and possibilities that our actions will be effective in meeting our goals. Our responsible choices flow from being enlightened about these possibilities and outcomes through social intelligence.

Although there is no precise definition of responsibility that can be applied to all social situations, in large part responsibility implies that we should do the best jobs we can, and at the same time consider the consequences of our behavior, and how they affect others as well as ourselves. Because social intelligence rests on the premises that we are social beings, and that we express our social awareness in all our actions, being responsible suggests that we need to honor our interdependency with others in whatever we undertake, including thinking about what we can do and what we will do.

Social intelligence helps us to discern the many ways in which we are connected to others, especially through our families, beliefs, social classes, cultures, and societies. Because we are interdependent in these different respects, we need to use a variety of ways of being connected to others. The webs of the relationships we construct, and participate in, define our opportunities to make responsible choices and act responsibly.

The higher level of awareness we attain, through increasing our social intelligence, requires that we pay attention to the broader social consequences of our actions, as well as their impacts on our lives and the lives of others. Our choices of how to be, and what to do, are not fully responsible until we have a fairly accurate idea of what those individual and social consequences may be. We must be able to predict, or at least understand, the most powerful social influences in our lives, if we are to aim for our goals and apply our strategies effectively and responsibly.

Although pondering these considerations does not sound like fun, in the long run we are inevitably faced with existential concerns about how we spend our lives, and which values we bring into being through our day-by-day actions. We do not have to answer to anyone other than ourselves, but we do need to make decisions about whether or not we assume some responsibilities for the well-being of those who are less privileged than we are, especially if we want to make meaningful contributions to others.

Social intelligence helps us to understand our own social advantages, and shows us how to give back some of the benefits we have received to those who have not had them. Deliberately orienting our lives, so that we aim more precisely at increasing social justice, for example, yields added purpose and direction. Doing this assures us that we are moving in constructive rather than destructive directions, and responsibility becomes an integral part of our choices to achieve social justice, and to make creative and lasting contributions to communities and societies.

Responsible choices also include taking collective actions, rather than depending solely on our individual preferences and strategies. Although we all make personal choices about our lifestyles and family exchanges, we also need to be able to work with others to accomplish complex, comprehensive tasks. In fact, we are the most responsible we can be when we become integral parts of collective efforts to accomplish social justice. We achieve more as team members, than when we act alone.

Past, Present, and Future

Social intelligence sharpens our perspectives on time. Not only do we heighten our awareness about the temper of the times in which we live by increasing our social intelligence, but we also deliberately use the past and present to create the future we want when we become historical actors. Our beliefs tie us to particular patterns of behavior and expectations related to the past, present, or future, and we increase our social intelligence when we coordinate these perspectives, so that we ultimately become more goal-directed, as well as more productive.

Understanding historical currents and flows of activity, as well as links between the past, present, and future, requires us to trace the cultural and emotional sources of traditions, which often bind us to repeat continuities in what we do and how we accomplish our goals. For example, we tend to have sentimental attachments to the past, just because this is our past, or we may choose to invest more feelings in our families, religions, or genders. Most people have strong emotional investments in particular social realities, such as religions or careers, because these life satisfactions are relatively scarce but highly rewarding.

In order to free ourselves for the present and the future, we need to think clearly about our commitments to the past, and to symbols of the past. We must find out what drives our strongest opinions, for example, and to what extent our sentiments about our own families block our understanding of significant patterns of interaction. Do our overly high expectations of what our families can do for us in modern societies prevent us from seeing the broader pictures of our lives? How can we change the less constructive aspects of our family beliefs?

Social intelligence is based on social facts, so that when we concentrate on increasing our social intelligence, we accumulate factual information about our varied beliefs. This provides a sufficiently solid foundation for deciding which of our beliefs should be continued from the past to the present and future, or which beliefs should be replaced by more realistic or more viable beliefs. We integrate our efforts to accomplish these goals by applying different time perspectives to our beliefs. For example, sizing up the time dimensions of our lives more accurately allows us to go forward with increased enthusiasm for either work or leisure.

An effective way to integrate our past, present, and future is to clarify the directions we want our lives to take. Social intelligence suggests that once we know where we want to go, merely heading in that direction will bring about different, but significant, adaptations. Turning our intentions and actions toward achieving social justice, for example, makes both our individual and collective efforts more effective, especially when we know what our starting points are as well as our destinations. We look closely at the past, in order to understand where we are coming from, so that we can fine tune our strategies of today for the future.

Exploring the starting points of our beliefs is both worthwhile and productive, as long as these tasks are undertaken carefully. We are not as effective in our actions when we head out intuitively in directions we like, as when we are truly prepared—by social intelligence—to set out on our specific journeys. Furthermore, once we set out, we have to be willing to rethink our strategies, especially if we realize that we are making superficial decisions rather than socially intelligent decisions.

It is hazardous to concentrate on the past so much that we lose ourselves in what was, rather than attend to what is and what could be. According to social intelligence, examining our past beliefs and past social conditions deepens our understanding of the power of our beliefs. Once this complex task is accomplished, however, the past should be put aside for a while, so that our energies can be more fully invested in forward-looking plans and actions.

Although it is difficult to move into vaguely defined futures, we can fairly easily decide to interact with members of younger generations, so that some wisdom from our past experiences is carried into the future. We can hone and discuss social intelligence with young adults, for example, because these principles are fairly easily learned by those who are open to new possibilities and applications. Maintaining concerns for the future, as well as creative ways to deal with the future as it approaches, are practical and helpful dimensions of increasing social intelligence. In these respects, social intelligence may fairly quickly prove itself to be an excellent orientation and preparation for our shared futures.

Ideally, we gradually link aspects of the past, present, and future to our complex ventures to achieve social justice. We persist in our efforts to increase our social intelligence, when we realize that this is a reliable and dependable way to make the world a better place. Thus social intelligence prepares us to take both individual and collective actions to increase opportunities to achieve social justice in our day-to-day lives.

Beliefs and Values

Our beliefs and values pervade our experiences, with the result that patterns of connection and association frequently emerge between our beliefs and our values. For example, our beliefs may reflect or strengthen our values; or our beliefs may lead us to change our values. Similarly, our values may predispose us to harbor specific beliefs, or reinforce our beliefs; and our values may lead us to change our beliefs.

Social intelligence suggests that if we want to know who we are, we should look at our values carefully, as well as at our beliefs. In doing this, a reliable methodology is to consider the substance of our beliefs as indicators of our values. What we believe yields content, which shows what our values are, as well as the extent to which our beliefs synthesize our community and societal values.

Increasing social intelligence involves discarding our less useful beliefs and replacing them with more productive beliefs. As we do this, we change priorities in our values. For example, we incorporate, or become more loyal to, values we treasure the most. Cultivating new values helps us to let go of values which we consider to be less useful or more harmful. Thus changing our beliefs, according to our personal preferences and social intelligence, ultimately means that we create opportunities to express different values.

Historically individuals, their communities, and their societies often had simpler belief systems, which had more direct associations between their beliefs and values. Being religious, for example, often suggested fairly clear correlations between what we believed and the values we honored, even though our social classes strongly influenced what our original and continuing choices of beliefs and values were. For instance, people believed in the value of discipline through their religions, especially when discipline was also a significant social class characteristic of parenting behavior and community standards.

Like beliefs, values are likely to be clustered in gestalts. Sometimes our clusters of beliefs overlap our clusters of values, and sometimes they are different from each other. For example, if we believe that freedom is an important condition of our optimal being, both our political beliefs and our political values influence how we define freedom. Social intelligence suggests that understanding the social conditions that characterize freedom makes us stronger and more effective, because we are more likely to place attaining freedom as a high priority in our day-to-day behavior.

Our beliefs and values predispose us either to accept the status quo or to innovate. Social intelligence encourages us to maintain critical postures to our beliefs and values, which allows us to innovate rather than merely accept the status quo. Social intelligence also suggests trajectories that aim to increase social justice, and require us to deliberately choose which beliefs and values to nurture.

Examinations of the social sources of our beliefs reveal many of the social sources of our values. They give us important information and direction about why we should accept or reject our beliefs and values. This strategy is necessary because, in order to deepen our commitments, we have to invest our passions and emotions in those beliefs and values which mean the most to us. This makes us more effective contributors to the common good, and increases meaning in our lives.

Sometimes we realize that our beliefs need fresh input from external influences. Our beliefs about honoring traditions, for example, are enlivened when we value learning as a way to both understand traditions and break with traditions. We are more likely to make successful innovations when we modify our past associations of beliefs and values, and use alternative values to inspire and inform new beliefs. Thus we are enlightened by values which do not reflect our prior beliefs, and we break new ground by considering and applying different values, with new priorities, to our situations. Cultural diversity, for example, involves the juxtaposition of values which have dramatic contrasts. Furthermore, being an historical actor shows us that valuing diversity is an important sea change in modern societies that we should recognize and live, especially as we increase social justice.

Because beliefs are our starting points in *Beliefs and Social Intelligence,* we consider beliefs here as having some degree of determining influence on our values. However, social intelligence loosens this hold of our beliefs somewhat, when we see how entertaining particular values predisposes us to formulate new beliefs, and to take innovative actions. Together our beliefs and values influence our individual and social changes in our families, communities, and societies. However, because modern cultures are forces to be reckoned with, we need to understand that our beliefs and values connect us to significant currents of constructive cultural change, as well as to patterns of cultural and social exploitation.

Focus

Social intelligence requires us to maintain a steady focus on ourselves and our social contexts. Enlarging our capacities to focus on social influences that affect us is a significant precondition for becoming more socially intelligent. This shift in our attention—away from our habitual ways of looking at ourselves and the world—is often difficult to achieve. However, we become more effectively focused through trial and error, and at the same time realize that we increase our social intelligence when we maintain our social systems focus on who we are and what we want to accomplish.

Focus involves giving our concentrated attention to the details of how we think, feel, and act, as well as to those patterns in our relationships and networks that affect us the most. Our social networks often have emotionally volatile past connections and influences, as well as strong impacts on our present and future connections and influences. Because we are social beings, we readily absorb others' expectations about our potentials and possibilities as our own. However, we need to maintain a stronger focus on those social influences that affect or limit us, before we can successfully redefine our situations. This also includes selecting those beliefs which reflect our most cherished values.

Being emotionally secure, and having adequate self respect, result from maintaining a strong focus on who we are and what we want to accomplish. When we understand others—and our attachments to them—more fully, we become more objective, as well as more able to withstand our everyday pressures to conform to their expectations. Developing and maintaining a clear and authentic sense of self is effective protection from becoming pawns in social influences, or amidst strong currents of social change and history. We increase our awareness of the necessarily fateful power of some of these social influences as we become more socially intelligent, so that we are more likely to be historical actors, as well as to increase social justice.

Some of the most challenging social pressures to withstand emanate from our families and intimate relationships. Although we want to love, to be loved, and to be accepted, we must above all cherish our integrity. For example, we try to act according to our own beliefs and priorities at all times, even when our strongest desires are in conflict with each other. These contradictions are minimized when we recognize that our beliefs and commitments are essential building blocks of who we are, and because they are at the core of our social intelligence. Our beliefs, and especially our commitments, define what we stand for, and how we conduct ourselves with others.

VI. Taking Charge of Beliefs

We are responsible only when we focus, and maintain our focus, on our beliefs, convictions, and commitments. Our personal integrity and social intelligence require and inspire us to act in accordance with our beliefs, convictions, and commitments as much as possible. However, unless we are wary and watchful about our social situations, we may be diverted from our good intentions.

Being focused helps us to stay the difficult course of becoming more socially intelligent, as well as to make the most of our lives by serving social justice ideals. We enjoy many aspects of our exchanges with others when we have purpose and direction, and actions that move us toward social justice give us important life satisfactions. We rescue our true selves as we develop our social intelligence, because we devote ourselves more wholeheartedly to increasing the common good. In spite of the difficulties and challenges involved in having this focus, we find that we lose nothing that really matters, and gain many meaningful rewards.

Social intelligence brings good cheer in our troubled times, as well as more specific, unexpected dividends. When we make the time and energy necessary to assess the social origins of our beliefs, substitute selected constructive beliefs for our destructive beliefs, and continue to focus on our beliefs, we avoid returning to our former ways of thinking and doing. Even though these processes are difficult, the more focused we are, the more successful our efforts will be, which allow social intelligence to protect us and enlighten our actions.

Focus ensures that we make more responsible choices, as well as helps us to link the past, the present, and the future more effectively in our actions. We take charge of our beliefs because we focus on them, and because we see crucial relationships between our beliefs and social values. Focus enables us to see ourselves and our worlds more clearly, and to envision viable alternatives, so that our social intelligence directs us to construct a better world for tomorrow.

Facts

We need to constantly check and validate our beliefs with social facts that result from expressing our beliefs. Although inevitably some, or even most, of our beliefs may refer to significant unknown aspects of our situations, which—like trends in globalization—may not seem to be directly related to our everyday lives, we should still collect and question facts related to our beliefs as much as we can. Our social intelligence is grounded in social facts, and because our beliefs need to be anchored in facts—to give us sufficient explanations, predictions, and guidance—we have to continuously observe and reflect about facts, in order to critically assess our beliefs.

Among our beliefs, clusters of religious beliefs are some of the most difficult beliefs to connect to facts. Even though we cannot reliably depend on religious devotions and rituals to shed light on complex worldly issues, we can use some facts to assess the extent to which we think our religious beliefs are reliable guides and inspirations.

We can compare, for example, what our lives are like with and without the guidance of our religious beliefs, and continue to identify these similarities or contrasts while we deal with current social realities. Also, comparing current facts with facts from our early years makes our assessments of the power of our religious beliefs more accurate. Facts also help us to assess the influences and effectiveness of specific religious beliefs.

Applications of our beliefs to resolve ongoing social problems, perhaps about our employment, are made more effective by gathering facts about the main players in these situations: for example, facts about their social classes, work histories, goals, and accomplishments. Facts clarify situations around employment issues, and enable us to develop more informed beliefs, and more informed ways of coping with unwanted social pressures or social stresses.

Both becoming and being socially intelligent require us to be alert to social facts about our families, beliefs, social classes, cultures, and societies. Reading serious daily newspapers, for example, shows us current social realities in our societies, and helps us to bring socially intelligent perspectives to bear on what we need to do as individuals and groups. Facts show us whether particular groups work together effectively to increase social justice, and help us to learn how we can be both enlightened and strategic in locating opportunities to work with groups we believe will achieve the most social justice.

One way to choose which group or groups to affiliate with is to examine factual records of groups which seem to be effective, well-organized, and productive. Facts from such groups can be compared and contrasted in light of our beliefs and expectations, referring to both our religious and secular beliefs whenever possible. This is useful because our religious beliefs and secular beliefs are often related to each other, and collecting facts about particular situations becomes a deciding factor in making commitments to increase the common good.

Both the facts of our lives, and the facts of our situations, help us to be honest about our beliefs and our behavior. If we want to make constructive contributions to societies, for example, all our beliefs must work for us. To the extent that we continue to harbor incompatible beliefs, which predictably produce conflicts and contradictions, we essentially neutralize—or at least sabotage—our efforts to attain our goals, even before we set out to accomplish them. Social intelligence helps us to use social facts as effective guides. For example, referring to social facts ensures that we become more effective in choosing and working with groups or organizations to increase social justice.

Because history is made up of accumulated facts, historical approaches to scrutinize how well our beliefs guide us are useful. For example, facts related to what we have achieved can be compared with facts about what we aimed to accomplish. When we use facts in these ways we are not day-dreaming, but rather grounding our realities in what has happened, and in what we predict could happen. Social intelligence makes us more knowledgeable about such practical possibilities. This means that we bring some of our ideals down to earth by making enlightened, sensible, workable, or sane decisions and commitments.

Relying on social facts to guide us helps us to take charge of our beliefs. Our beliefs are more reliable when they are tested with facts, rather than allowed to drive us or divert us from achieving our most cherished goals and values. Facts discipline our beliefs by keeping us on track to reach our goals. At the same time, facts ensure that we move toward social justice, and increase our life satisfactions.

VII. Beliefs as Motivation

Optimally we act according to our deliberately constructed motivations, rather than react to our most powerful emotions or passions of the moment. Furthermore, at best, our most cherished individual and social beliefs move us to act, especially when we think through what it is that we want to accomplish, and how we can contribute to the common good. Because social justice is a social ideal, cultivating our beliefs about social justice leads us toward both increasing social justice and experiencing individual and social fulfillment.

When we take charge of our beliefs through increasing our social intelligence, we become more motivated by our chosen beliefs, than by the contradictory beliefs we had previously, often due to our families' or significant others' vested interests. As we continue to deliberately select and refine our beliefs, we become more strongly motivated to accomplish tasks which yield a higher good, than if we had not increased our social intelligence.

Social intelligence helps us not only to increase the efficiency of our beliefs as motivations, but also to strengthen our motivations. We have greater stamina to deal with obstacles that stand in our way, for example, when we keep our beliefs oriented toward our ideals, yet at the same time remain firmly based in social realities. Social intelligence shows us how to ground our beliefs in social facts, so that we continue to be both practical and responsible in making our everyday decisions and commitments.

Understanding these links between our beliefs, motives, and actions frees us to envision the most constructive social possibilities to neutralize some of the difficulties we inevitably face as we go about our daily business. First, by giving our attention to our family beliefs, and then by scrutinizing our religious, social class, cultural, and societal beliefs, we heighten our awareness about social influences, social interactions, and social intelligence in all our actions. This prepares us to do the best we can, in a world full of complex social issues and social dilemmas.

When we continue to cultivate our social awareness, and persist in refining the deliberateness of our actions as historical actors, we ensure that we make responsible choices. Consequently, we carve out pathways that more predictably bring about increased social justice, as well as ways to share meaningful social satisfactions. Developing social intelligence guarantees that we do what we can to create a better world for more people, for example, so that we herald and embrace diversity rather than ethnocentrism in our transactions with others.

Knowing how we, our communities, and our societies link our past, present, and future helps us to neutralize some of our shared tendencies to become bigoted in our family, religious, and political beliefs. Social intelligence fortifies us amidst the disconcerting pressures and dislocations of rapid social changes, and helps us to adjust and adapt to the social stresses around and within us.

Because our beliefs are our motivations, whether we realize this or not, we inevitably test out our beliefs as we act in the world. When we see and understand which of our beliefs withstand criticisms and experiential facts, for example, we distinguish more clearly how our beliefs connect us to our values. Furthermore, understanding our beliefs more fully helps us to realize the particular values we honor through our beliefs, so that we see how we deepen our connections to traditions through our beliefs, even though we may not intend to do this.

VII. Beliefs as Motivation

Our heightened awareness of social intelligence illumines how we use beliefs and values in our everyday lives, as well as how we participate in ongoing sea changes of values in our societies. Social intelligence makes us realize the importance of harboring our most constructive social beliefs as motivations, and the necessity to discard our destructive social beliefs. Our capacities to make decisions along these lines are strengthened as we increase our social intelligence, because we become more adept at understanding the outcomes of our value choices. We also develop a fuller appreciation of the wide variety of challenges we predictably encounter as we continue to make value choices.

Maintaining our focus on deliberately selecting our beliefs, and on the trial and error testing of our beliefs with social facts, ensures that we stay the course and sustain our motivations to accomplish goals which meet our real needs and increase social justice. Unless we develop constructive motivations, we cannot accomplish our most productive individual and collective actions. This focus on the qualities of our beliefs as motivations, and their connections to values and social realities, makes our lives more socially intelligent.

Becoming an Historical Actor

Seeing ourselves as historical actors changes our perspectives, and gives us broader vantage points from which to view our everyday worlds. Social intelligence is based on selecting broad social contexts to understand the power of social influences in our particular situations, and this understanding becomes a foundation for motivating our behavior as historical actors. Thus increasing social intelligence makes us more effective historical actors.

Becoming and being historical actors does not necessarily mean that we have to be heroic in our deeds, or recognized leaders in our communities or societies. Rather, we need to acknowledge that we are all historical actors, whether we know it or not, because we cannot avoid the push and pull of strong historical influences in the long run, and because each decision we make has some impact on others as well as ourselves. Due to the fact that anything that anyone does in both private and public arenas has social consequences, we are historical actors in spite of ourselves.

Social intelligence is based on the empirical principles that we do not act in vacuums; our behavior reflects or expresses our specific social situations; and major social influences strongly affect our beliefs and whatever we do. Social intelligence also suggests that the strongest social influences on our beliefs and on our behavior derive from our families, religions, social classes, cultures, and societies. Because of the power of these principles of social intelligence, *Beliefs and Social Intelligence* helps us to discover the social origins of our beliefs, as well as how social intelligence clarifies our beliefs, so that we can increase the meaningfulness and effectiveness of our impacts on our worlds today and in the future.

Social intelligence shows us that, as historical actors, we need to take our decision-making and actions seriously. The breadth of vision of social intelligence helps us to acknowledge our latent and manifest powers as historical actors, so that we respond more appropriately to the pragmatic reality that we are historical actors, whether we wish this was so or not. Thus social intelligence helps us to be clearer and more honest about the nature of human nature, and the scope of our actual and possible influences on each other.

However, because social intelligence suggests that we are all historical actors, we immediately see that the responsibility for taking strategic social actions does not rest only on our own shoulders. When we believe that others, as well as ourselves, are historical actors, we understand that taking collective action is a more powerful means of bringing about constructive social changes than individual actions, as well as of making changes that last into the future. Because the forces of social change are relentlessly complex, and the tasks involved in bringing about social changes are difficult or challenging, we need to know how to cooperate with others in order to be effective.

Becoming historical actors, through increasing our social intelligence, not only emphasizes the practical necessities of working collectively to achieve shared goals of social change, especially when they are oriented toward social justice, but also introduces new orientations to history. For example, in the past many histories reported the selective triumphs of social or political elites. By contrast, social intelligence perspectives on history emphasize grass roots efforts to bring about social changes, including those which go beyond the achievements of organized social movements.

We work effectively with others for a wide variety of purposes. For example, highly organized groups, such as major corporations, are sustained by shared beliefs, values, roles, and responsibilities. We need to assess how social intelligence and becoming historical actors directs us to work in particular groups, and how socially intelligent ways of working differ from the more ritualized interactions found in conventional organizations. We have to determine for ourselves, for example, why it is worth our while to become more socially intelligent, so that we assume responsibilities as historical actors in collective social change ventures.

In order to assess whether the beliefs that lead us to take collective actions are more or less socially intelligent, we examine the specific goals of groups and their collective actions, as well as our own intentions. After scrutinizing these objectives, we make our assessments in light of socially intelligent principles: for example, goals which move us toward increasing social justice are more socially intelligent than goals based solely on boosting revenues and increasing profits.

In order to become aware historical actors, we cultivate beliefs which show us how to think beyond achieving our own self-interests, especially if we are to be socially intelligent in our individual and collective actions. Making our own self-interests our highest priority is not characteristic of socially intelligent historical actors, and frequently leads toward decreasing rather than increasing social justice in the long run. By contrast, when we work toward increasing our social intelligence, we recognize that we are historical actors, and that we can act to increase the common good for all. In these respects, our ultimate goals as historical actors are often for our societies to become more egalitarian, inclusive, diverse, cooperative, and open, rather than more competitive or more conflicted.

Responsible Choices

When we realize that our beliefs motivate us to act, we see that becoming an aware historical actor helps us to take well-integrated, purposeful actions, which may transcend our minute-by-minute choices. However, given the fact that widely different social influences are significant contexts of our lives, we need to understand which of our many beliefs motivate us the most. Because social intelligence makes us aware that we are historical actors, making responsible choices means that we act to increase social justice. Thus our choices are more or less responsible compared with our ideal to increase the common good for all, and we need to choose how to be more responsible through our everyday decisions.

Because responsible choices are often experienced as being overly serious in our contemporary hedonistic, fun-loving cultures, the benefits of making responsible choices may not be widely known, felt, or explored. The goals or ideals of responsible choices often seem to be highly disciplined options that are not preferred by most people—perhaps being thought of as others' choices rather than our own. Given this general resistance to making responsible choices, one step toward tuning in more satisfactorily to what our responsible choices are, is to make sure that we are authentic in making our choices.

VII. Beliefs as Motivation

Being responsible helps us to fulfill our missions to be historical actors. Even though everyone is an historical actor, we are often unaware of this fact. However, when we learn about the power and complexity of broad social influences, as well as about social justice, at the same time that we increase our social intelligence, we are more responsible for the outcomes of our actions. When we are not socially intelligent, we tend to act in isolation from others, by denying crucial links between our world views and our actions.

Responsible choices of beliefs are socially intelligent. They motivate actions that have constructive impacts on others, through incorporating our individual and social heritages as historical actors. Responsible choices of beliefs are also reliable means to make our most constructive contributions to the common good. We listen to others more carefully, for example, when we make responsible choices in our beliefs, so that our decisions lead us to contribute to the common good more effectively.

If we choose not to pay close attention to social influences, we cannot be socially intelligent. Consequently, when we are not sufficiently socially intelligent to know whether we are making responsible choices, we are usually not sufficiently motivated to increase the common good. This chain of conditions suggests that our choices are predictably more responsible when we are socially intelligent. However, because the ways in which we are socially intelligent vary, we know that one responsible choice is to commit ourselves to continue to work toward increasing our social intelligence.

Social intelligence shows us that our responsible choices depend on social influences in our families, religions, social classes, cultures, and societies. Our beliefs and motivations result from the degree of our understanding of these influences, as well as from the social tensions we experience in relation to them. Consequently, we move toward social justice, or away from social justice, as we make our daily decisions.

In sum, taking charge of our beliefs enables us to take charge of our motives and actions. When we make responsible choices about which social beliefs we entertain and nurture, we also decide which social beliefs will formulate our ideals and goals. When we use social intelligence to choose our motivations more deliberately, we are more effective historical actors in our families, communities, and societies. Because social intelligence enables us to predict the consequences of our actions more precisely, we can motivate ourselves to make responsible choices. This increases our effectiveness in accomplishing our goals and social justice.

Our responsible choices allow us to integrate different aspects of our past, present, and future social influences through our beliefs and values. Furthermore, our chosen values reinforce our beliefs and motivations to act. We continue to check the reliability of our beliefs, through examining the facts of our social situations, so that we maintain our focus on responsible choices, and apply social intelligence to all aspects of our lives.

Past, Present, and Future

Our motivations for our behavior in the here and now need to be directly related to our present circumstances to some extent. If our beliefs are overly attached to either the past or the future, for example, we cannot be sufficiently grounded in our present realities, and our behavior is predictably less effective than it could be. Ideally—that is, when we are sufficiently free to give some attention to the past, present, and future—we choose social beliefs that reflect our vested interests in these different orientations to time.

Just as our patterns of behavior, relationships, and commitments need some degree of flexibility, our beliefs need some degree of attachment to the past, present, and future. If we are oriented only to the past, we inevitably miss considerable opportunities of the day, as well as numerous possibilities for defining future developments in our particular situations. Social intelligence requires us to continue to cultivate our awareness of major social influences and social conditions in the past, present, and future, in order to understand the power and complexity of these social forces in our lives.

When we pay attention to past, present, and future social influences, we understand our circumstances more fully, and produce more integrated responses to our situations. In order to be responsible in our choices as historical actors, we must consider both continuities and inconsistencies in how we go about accomplishing our goals. This focus helps us to substitute more constructive beliefs for more destructive beliefs as motivations to act. Ultimately, enlightenment means seeing ourselves and others in a variety of social and cultural contexts, so that we can truly avail ourselves of multiple possibilities.

When we innovate or envision future possibilities in difficult situations, we have to come to terms with social influences of the past, present, and future. For example, we deliberately motivate ourselves to act through connecting ourselves with past, present, and future social influences, so that our goals are more universally applicable, and our historical perspectives are more widely recognized. Our contributions reach larger groups of people when we incorporate broad perspectives of the past, present, and future in our beliefs, motives, and behavior.

Being an historical actor does not mean that we orient our vision and behavior solely to the past. Rather, we recognize the historical roots of our present situations, act with a sound knowledge of the present, and at the same time have keen perceptions of future possibilities. We maintain this comprehensive or global perspective on time, in order to bring it to bear on our decisions and behavior in different places. We are historical actors because we see beyond the immediacy of the present, and consider both the past and the future in our current beliefs, motivations, and actions.

In some respects our actions must be rooted most deeply in our present social realities, because we exist now. However, being able to predict the consequences of our present behavior necessarily includes having sufficient knowledge of the past, as well as some capacity to estimate future conditions. Ideally, this breadth of our past, present, and future perspectives permeates all of our beliefs and motives, so that the consequences of our actions become more compelling, as well as more socially useful. We are more effective historical actors, more responsible decision-makers, and more fulfilled people when we consider our interests and actions in these broad time perspectives.

Social intelligence guides and encourages us to balance our perspectives on time, so that we can develop more accurate assessments of where we are in time and place, and make more effective contributions to increasing social justice and the common good. Social intelligence enlarges the capacities of our beliefs to motivate us to act, by enriching the meanings of our social situations through past, present, and future perspectives.

Social intelligence further fuels the effectiveness of our behavior through linking our beliefs and motivations to social values, which allows us to have stronger impacts on the past, present, and future. Our awareness of our values, as historical actors, enables us to focus more precisely on specific ideals of social justice. At the same time that we do this, we check social realities in our outcomes, through examining the changing social facts of our situations according to our past, present, and future concerns.

Beliefs and Values

We benefit from choosing which beliefs we want to guide us, as well as the values for which we want to live and strive. If we believe that we need freedom, for example, in order to survive in our families, and in order to inspire our community contributions, we must commit ourselves to pursuing freedom as a value in society. Even though there are many occasions when societal values are too vague to be used as specific guides, we find that if we move in the general direction of a particular social value, we become more motivated to accomplish goals related to that value.

In these respects our value choices reflect and reinforce our chosen substantive beliefs. Social intelligence helps us to clarify these important decisions, so that we exercise our autonomy, not only over our choices of beliefs, but also over our choices of values. Because our beliefs are often more deeply internalized than our values, which are usually less personal, making commitments to particular values may be more of a public statement than deciding which of our beliefs to honor. Also, as we strengthen our allegiances to our chosen beliefs, our values often flow more or less automatically from our selected beliefs.

Social justice can be viewed as a social value as well as a social ideal. Social intelligence helps us to choose our beliefs; allows these beliefs to motivate our goals and actions; and guides our choices of social justice values. However, we should not commit ourselves to social justice values unless we are ready to orient our day-to-day behavior toward goals that move us in this direction. Although following a trajectory toward social justice is expected when we increase our social intelligence, this is not automatic, and should not be undertaken until we have made considerable adjustments in our beliefs and values.

Our values are different from our specific beliefs in that they are more rooted in societies and offer us broader vistas. They are significant for strengthening our beliefs because they enable us to share similar ideals and orientations with more people. Even though there may not be a great deal of agreement about what our specific beliefs about education are, for example, most of us can value education in general, because we often agree about shared concerns like the value of education for all people, the value of education at young or old ages, and the value of continuing our education for a lifetime.

Where our beliefs are clustered, as in religions, they not only motivate us to act in a wide variety of contrasting situations, but they also orient us to particular values like hard work, family traditions, independence, or obedience. However, when we are more selective about our religious beliefs, perhaps by not accepting entire clusters of religious beliefs uncritically, we necessarily change our allegiances to some traditional values, and become more discriminating about our present and future value choices. Our beliefs and values are powerful motivators, but they are not fixed and rigid. We can change our own beliefs and values at any time; modify their patterns of mutuality and interdependence; or work toward changing values in particular societies.

Choosing our values affects our selections of beliefs. When we become historical actors we may be more aware of our values than our beliefs, for example, so that changes in our behavior develop from changing our values rather than from changing our beliefs. However, whatever sequences emerge in the development of our values and beliefs, our values, beliefs, and daily practices continue to be major forces in our lives, and they ultimately feed into our actions and achievements in our cultures and societies.

We see some of the more dramatic individual and social consequences of changing our beliefs and values more clearly when we understand how religious conversion or intensive education transforms lives. We open up new vistas when we connect our beliefs to values, or when we allow social values to guide our selections of beliefs.

Social intelligence encourages us to make these significant decisions through examining our first-hand experiences of beliefs and values, and through seeing the impacts that our beliefs and values have on the changing facts of our social situations. When we know, through these experiential tests, that particular beliefs or values serve us well, we become more socially intelligent by honoring beliefs and values that make us who we want to be, and help us to accomplish what we want to achieve.

Focus

In order to sharpen and strengthen our motivations, we need to clarify and synchronize our social beliefs. We do this by understanding as much as we can about the social origins of our beliefs, and the history of our beliefs. Social intelligence helps to discern which of our beliefs are more salient for our personal and community fulfillment. Furthermore, giving our attention to our most meaningful beliefs enables us to refine these beliefs to motivate us.

These processes of probing research, analysis, and commitment make the cores of our social beliefs more intelligible and more meaningful. Linking our reactions in social situations to these beliefs helps us to focus on the strongest social influences in our situations, so that our social intelligence guides us ever more clearly toward taking constructive actions. This level of awareness about our beliefs gives us an invaluable focus, which necessarily goes beyond self-interest, because it is grounded in social intelligence and social justice.

When everything we think, say, and do is permeated by social awareness and social know-how, we inevitably accomplish more through our actions. Our focuses on our beliefs, and on our current situations, allow us to use socially intelligent principles to develop constructive interactions with others. Also, because our chosen beliefs are our motives, our social intelligence ensures that our most valued social ideals guide us, and allow us to at least partially transcend the unavoidable hurdles of everyday life. Thus focus adds meaning to our actions, so that we are more likely to sustain our efforts and fulfill the goals we set for ourselves.

The power of our capacities to focus enables us to withstand the many distractions that inevitably come our way. We save our energies and resources when we go in one overall direction, for example, rather than in ten different directions, so that each of our decisions and actions counts for more. When we are socially intelligent, we focus on social justice more effectively, because we are more immune to ideals and goals which do not strengthen our missions to increase the common good for all.

Sharpening our focus in this way also helps us to be more aware of our assumptions and what we take for granted. Even when we think we know what we are about, some of our most deep-seated assumptions will surface, especially those which we do not usually consider very seriously. The emergence of this deeper layer of our assumptions provides further opportunities to make choices about our hidden beliefs, which again refines our focus and effectiveness.

Focusing on our in-depth, hidden beliefs makes us more responsible and more effective at linking past, present, and future time dimensions in our thinking, planning, and actions. As historical actors, our focuses increase our confidence and effectiveness, so that we make more responsible choices. This is accomplished because we understand the consequences of our actions more reliably, and more fully, before we undertake them.

Assessing how we focus our attention is useful in identifying our ongoing beliefs and motives. All too often we allow ourselves to be influenced by other people, so that we reduce our awareness of our own goals and motives. Also, when we get too swept away by connecting our beliefs with social values, we may head toward broad vistas which seem to be meaningful, but which may not be directly related to our more immediate or more specific chosen goals.

Focusing on social realities saves our lives as well as our energies. Checking to what extent social facts result from our actions is consistently important, for example. Understanding our social beliefs and motives ensures that we live as fully as possible, and that we are leading our own lives rather than those of other people. We see that we become more distinctive in our thinking and doing when we focus on staying fully awake to opportunities and possibilities. Paying attention to how we focus, and what we focus on, enables us to be more active— rather than passive—in our responsiveness to our families, communities, and societies.

When we maintain our focus on our beliefs and motives, our work toward increasing social justice and the common good becomes an increasingly important component of how we behave on a daily basis, and of how we increase our social intelligence. When our beliefs and motives are grounded in social awareness, and we recognize the power of social facts in our ongoing situations, sustaining a focus on our goals enhances our effectiveness, and ultimately increases social justice.

Facts

Unlike other sources of intelligence and wisdom, social intelligence derives from social facts. When we are socially intelligent our beliefs are constantly checked against the facts of our actual social conditions, so that our social intelligence consists largely of paying attention to what these facts tell us, rather than just to what our beliefs suggest. By attaining this kind of objectivity and reverence for facts, we do not deny beliefs' compelling powers over our motives, but rather make sure that we are well-informed about the ways in which our beliefs and values are related to our social realities.

Focusing on facts is central to social intelligence. The facts of our social intelligence allow us to be more flexible and more adaptive than we could be, for example, if we insisted on harboring beliefs about being morally right in all circumstances. We cannot afford to close our minds to practical, factual sources of information about our social conditions and social influences, because facts give us continuing control over our beliefs and decisions to act. Our ideals of open social systems, diverse communities, and inclusive definitions of the common good all depend on checking our most cherished beliefs with the social facts of our situations, if we are to be socially intelligent in our actions.

Knowing that we are strongly influenced by our families, beliefs, social classes, cultures, and societies, we become more adept at taking charge of the impacts of these social forces on our lives, when we observe and interpret social facts which deepen our knowledge and understanding of families, beliefs, social classes, cultures, and societies. These facts become foundations for using social intelligence to guide our decisions and actions. We only appreciate the necessity for social intelligence and its compelling qualities, when we understand the facts of our families, beliefs, social classes, cultures, and societies, as well as how they vary through time and place.

Each person has a unique set of social circumstances. When we are aware of the range of possibilities in others' situations as well as our own, we assess more objectively and more accurately what minimum and optimum conditions could and should be maintained for all people. Starting with such practical standards of how societies actually meet human needs helps us to achieve social justice. We should ask ourselves, for example, which facts in existing social conditions allow whole populations to be relatively free of conflict and strife? Which facts show us the quality of education we need, in order to encourage and preserve beliefs that allow us to survive and be fulfilled? How do facts show us what our social obligations are to others, especially given the widely varying social circumstances in different societies?

Facts open up possibilities for thinking through and discussing social justice issues, as well as realistic goals and expectations. Facts help us to make more objective inventories of our resources, more adequate distributions of resources in societies, and more realistic assessments of special needs for resources. By virtue of being members of particular societies, we are involuntarily plunged into restless seas of reciprocity.

VII. Beliefs as Motivation

When we are socially intelligent, we realize that we are responsible actors only when we come to terms with—or deal with—the complexity of the social facts of these social realities.

Just as in choosing which beliefs we want to honor, which beliefs we will release, or which beliefs increase our motivations the most, collecting facts about the substance and consequences of our beliefs enables us to further assess and control how our beliefs influence our lives. Looking at facts related to goals we want to achieve, for example, as well as hopes and expectations embodied in our beliefs, enables us to determine whether we are on the right tracks to accomplish these goals and increase social justice.

We cannot afford to ignore or distort the social facts of our situations. We are more objective, as well as more socially intelligent, when we depend on facts to make our decisions and commitments. Using facts to interpret our social circumstances makes our motives clearer and stronger, and our beliefs become more reliable in guiding us to attain greater personal and collective satisfactions. By contrast, denying the facts of our social situations decreases our social intelligence, so that we gradually become victims of our social circumstances. These are handicaps that we should definitively avoid if we are to meet and fulfill our most cherished goals and dreams.

VIII. Orientations to Action

O ur orientations to action necessarily focus on ourselves and the world, even though we may not be aware of what our orientations are. For example, our orientations show us where we are going, as well as what we expect from others. Ideally, we orient our actions according to forward-looking postures of what could be, rather than backward-looking views of what has been. Our orientations to action encourage us to innovate more effectively when they are rooted in what exists in the present, or in what could be in the future, than in what was in the past.

Social intelligence shows us how our thinking and imagining emerge from the past, present, and future, as well as grounds us in as many social facts as possible from the past, present, and future. Social intelligence also connects us to specific places and times, so that we maintain as much control as possible in how we orient or strategize our actions.

Although we cannot be certain about the behavioral outcomes of our actions, we predict the results of our behavior more accurately when we are aware of our orientations, rather than if we act randomly or with mixed thoughts and attitudes. Just as our beliefs give us reasons to act, which most importantly motivate us to act or not to act, the beliefs we use as orientations to action help us guide our behavior more precisely. For example, we may choose to direct our actions toward achieving global social justice in the future or toward achieving present well-being in a particular community.

Both our motives and orientations are made up largely of our beliefs. We not only need to nurture beliefs which are compatible with our taking action, but also beliefs which direct us toward achieving the specific goals we want to attain. Social intelligence shows us how to become more aware of our beliefs, how to refine them, how to select them, how to increase or decrease them, and how to use them in ways which we really choose. In addition to clarifying our choices of beliefs, social intelligence helps us to understand the social facts of our situations, to know the social consequences of holding particular beliefs, and to check social facts in the consequences of our beliefs. Making these assessments ensures that we orient our actions as precisely as possible toward our preferred goals.

Using social intelligence to guide our orientations to actions also reminds us that we are more effective when we act collectively, rather than in isolation from others. We can therefore surmise that whenever possible we should act in concert with others, rather than alone, in order to have a greater impact on our communities and societies. This means that we need to develop strategies for orientations to actions which increase our effectiveness in reaching collective goals.

Therefore, although social intelligence increases our motivations to make community contributions as historical actors, we also need to make sure that our actions are oriented as directly as possible toward the particular goals we want to accomplish. Our outcomes are in large part determined by the quality and integrity of our social beliefs, so we must continue to be cautious about the social origins of our beliefs, as well as their impacts on how we think and what we do.

The good news about the power of our beliefs—as motivations and orientations for our actions—is that because our beliefs are learned, they can be changed. Because there is nothing genetic or fixed about our beliefs, we have myriad choices and opportunities to change our beliefs whenever we want to do so. This freedom in our choices of beliefs is restricted only by the level of our social intelligence. Continuing to increase our social intelligence ensures that we find or make adaptations that work well for us and others.

Carefully selecting beliefs as orientations to our actions makes our choices and decisions more responsible. We increase the clarity of the intent of our actions by using past, present, and future orientations for our actions, as well as by linking our beliefs and values more coherently and more deliberately. We pay attention to our choices of beliefs by focusing on the impacts of those social influences that affect us the most, and by collecting as many social facts as possible about our present and continuing situations.

Our major safeguard in these complex processes, and in our capacities to formulate adequate orientations for our actions, is our continuing goal of increasing our social intelligence. The integrity and coordination of our actions increase when we apply principles of social intelligence to our identities and actions, so that we remain more consistent and more effective in our strategies and outcomes. Ultimately, social intelligence guides us toward achieving social justice, which means that we add personal and social satisfactions at the same time that we increase our individual and collective social intelligence.

Becoming an Historical Actor

Becoming an historical actor is a fairly advanced stage of being socially intelligent. However, the more preliminary stages of understanding the complexity of social influences and social beliefs—such as those found in our families, religions, social classes, cultures, and societies—cannot be forgotten or ignored. In fact, we often need to return to these basic steps of becoming socially intelligent, especially if we want to be socially intelligent on a continuing basis when we are historical actors. Once we understand social influences more fully, we become more deliberate historical actors, who consistently and persistently pursue social justice goals, as well as use and increase social intelligence.

When we are aware historical actors, we are more able to use our social knowledge of the past effectively, in order to orient our present actions to the future. As we do this, we assess sufficient social facts about our present situations, so that we can predict at least some of the most significant future consequences of our actions as accurately as possible. At the same time that we orient our actions toward present and future circumstances, we need to understand the social contexts of our actions and our societies as much as possible. This enables us to continue to cultivate our historical awareness, as well as to act constructively in relation to established currents of historical change.

Sharing our goals and identities as historical actors with others also requires that we continue to see connections between our orientations to actions and the outcomes of our actions. This helps us to act more effectively as individuals, groups, and societies. Social intelligence directs us to make collective decisions, and take collective actions, whenever possible, because cooperating with others helps us to accomplish more than acting individually, in relative isolation from others. Although many—perhaps even most—people do not deliberately orient their actions, we need to know that we are inevitably historical actors, whether we realize this or not. This means that it helps us to pay attention to how the impacts of our actions are predictably limited or expanded by our inward-looking or outward-looking orientations to life.

When we are socially intelligent, we may decide that one of our social justice missions is to heighten others' awareness about the choices they make in orienting their world views and actions. Even though collective actions have more social impact and import than individual acts, individual decisions and actions also have marked effects on outcomes. This makes it even more imperative that we act from the starting point of having deliberately selected our most cherished beliefs as our orientations to action. When people are persuaded that their actions can make the world a better place, and that how they orient their lives has a strong impact on the effectiveness of their contributions, they are more motivated to explore what their real choices are in selecting beliefs to create meaningful orientations.

Realizing that we can change our beliefs strengthens our seriousness of purpose in choosing our motivations and orientations. Understanding how we form and perpetuate our beliefs frees us from chains of predictable negative or destructive consequences, which result from closing our minds to our most constructive possibilities. Above all it is important to stay open-minded to our individual and collective options in these critical associations and sequences of events.

Social intelligence guides us to select beliefs that work best for us as orientations to our actions in our daily exchanges, and in pursuing social justice. Believing in the importance of increasing our social intelligence fuels these processes, so that we become more committed and more effective as historical actors. As a result, we are more responsible in our choices; more knowledgeable about the past, present, and future; more resourceful in how we link our beliefs and values; and more effective in our work with others to achieve socially intelligent goals.

Our increased familiarity with the principles of social intelligence sharpens our awareness of the importance of clarifying our orientations and working toward increasing social justice. For example, we are more adept at focusing on what we think we should be doing, as well as at absorbing sufficient social facts about our particular situations. Furthermore, when being an historical actor is an individual and social reality, we become historical actors in wider ranges of social settings, and our overall impacts are increased.

Responsible Choices
We are responsible when we choose to learn as many social facts as possible about our situations, and choose to act to bring

about constructive rather than destructive changes. We are also responsible when we choose to nurture beliefs which envision an expanded common good, rather than beliefs which focus on competition for narrow, self-interested goals.

When we make these kinds of broad-ranging responsible choices in accepting or rejecting our own beliefs, we are considerably more effective in our actions than if we look only at the social circumstances around us. Because our beliefs orient our behavior, they are the substance of the impacts of our actions. If we are not accomplishing our goals, we need to make more responsible choices in our beliefs by changing them.

Other responsible choices, from the point of view of our beliefs and social intelligence, consist of continuing to learn about the most powerful social influences in our lives, as well as collecting as many facts as possible about these influences. For example, in addition to reflecting about our own social experiences, we should understand as much as we can about families, beliefs, social classes, cultures, and societies. Compiling a detailed knowledge about these powerful social and emotional influences allows us assess important contexts of our behavior.

When we have investigative priorities, social intelligence helps us to see the overall power and complexity of social influences in our situations. For example, we deliberately cultivate a realistic reverence for social forces as we make responsible choices in our beliefs, orientations, decisions, and behavior. Also, we know that we are who we are largely due to social influences, and due to our beliefs about these influences.

Comparing social facts with our beliefs, and making sure that our beliefs reflect important social realities in our situations, keep us sufficiently aware to make responsible choices. We need to continue to apply these disciplined observations to our everyday lives, however, if we are to achieve those individual and social goals which we cherish the most. We cannot be productive if we use the principles of social intelligence only once in a while, or haphazardly. Rather, we need to stay alert to the power of social forces at all times. We are responsible when we keep our awareness of social influences uppermost in our priorities, as well as at the back of our minds at all times. When we lose track of the necessity of using principles of social intelligence to orient our behavior, we succumb to the more destructive powers of social influences, as well as lose control over the consequences of our actions.

Social intelligence encourages us to find meaningful ways to act collectively rather than individually. When we realize that we are more effective if we work with others who share our goals, we begin to veer away from focusing solely on our own accomplishments, even if these increase social justice.

Thus social intelligence encourages us to work with others for pragmatic rather than moral reasons. Pooling our thinking and resources with others increases our efficiency, because teams of workers can increase our capacities to make more organized, focused efforts. Due to these facts of the human condition, we are more responsible when we choose to work with others, rather than choose to work in isolation from others.

Becoming an aware historical actor occurs only when we have achieved a fairly high level of social intelligence. This orientation strengthens our capacities to increase diversity through our responsible choices. One of the most characteristic responsible choices of being an historical actor is to use information from the past, present, and future in decision-making, especially when undertaking difficult tasks collectively, in order to increase social justice. Our later successes in accomplishing our enlightened collective goals also depend on making responsible decisions.

Beliefs which support responsible choices are often linked to particular values. For example, we enter into societal discourse more readily when we identify social values which support social justice—such as equality, inclusiveness, diversity, cooperation, or openness—and when we develop value-focused strategies to work collaboratively with others.

Our responsible choices may orient us toward starting or developing grassroots social movements, at the same time that we continue to work toward achieving more specific goals. Because social intelligence suggests that we pursue social justice for pragmatic or idealistic reasons, we may usefully find broad social support for our objectives. However, whatever our working conditions are, the facts of our social situations change as we increase social justice, so that our responsible choices must also protect our constructive social networks from being destroyed.

Past, Present, and Future

Becoming historical actors, through making responsible choices, necessarily coordinates our views of the past, present, and future as meaningful orientations to our actions. Because our most enlightened, most factually informed decisions flow from those beliefs which orient us to ourselves, others, and the world, what we believe about the past, present, and future influences how we see our situations, how we think, and what we choose to do.

Although it is undoubtedly important to live in the present—so that we feel truly alive and live fully—we are more thoughtful about social issues in our day-to-day behavior when we also consider the past and future. We should know, for example, how our pasts are connected to our present, as well as what futures may be possible. How do our present circumstances reflect our pasts? To what extent do our future possibilities depend on our pasts and the present? How do our beliefs about the passage of time affect our views of the present, and our assessments of future possibilities? Also, how do we go about changing our orientations to time in our actions if we are unrealistic in our expectations for the present and future?

One of the most significant links between our beliefs and our orientations to our actions is holding negative views of possible futures, which limits our capacities to have constructive impacts on the future. However, when we understand our beliefs and their consequences sufficiently to see that our orientations to our actions may restrict our options for improving our futures, we realize sooner or later that we need to cultivate more constructive beliefs as orientations to our actions, in order to create opportunities for constructive changes. It is not enough merely to have sufficient beliefs to motivate us to accomplish changes. We also need to nurture beliefs which orient us more directly to take specific actions, to design successful strategies, and to assess the extent to which we are accomplishing significant changes.

Social intelligence encourages us to balance our beliefs about the past, present, and future, so that our orientations to actions are as objective as possible. Even though our lived experiences yield deep-seated views of social realities, beliefs derived from our own experiences are necessarily biased, and even prejudiced, to some extent. This means that we need to collect additional information from other sources about our social situations, in order to be more objective.

When we are balanced and objective in orienting our actions to the past, present, and future, we become more adept at assessing the extent to which we view the future positively. Even though focusing on the past and present are vital ways to understand our situations, because this helps us to define our starting points more accurately, we also need to aim our actions meaningfully and effectively through choosing constructive beliefs about the future. Unless we approach the future with interest and thoughtfulness, we inevitably tend to be backward-looking in our concerns and emphases. Consequently, because there are so many problematic issues in our current worlds, we cannot afford to minimize the pragmatic significance of increasing the common good and social justice for future well-being.

When we ponder the roles that our beliefs play in orienting our actions toward achieving more productive futures, we realize that we need to remain flexible and open to new possibilities. This belief is shared, to some extent, by others who try to live according to social intelligence principles. We respond to the future most effectively, for example, when we stay open to possibilities which we cannot easily imagine or understand today. Also, because we need to act in concert with others, we continue to orient our actions to achieve social justice in as many future situations as possible.

History shows us that unless we make deliberate interventions to articulate particular values, or achieve specific goals, societies tend to repeat what existed in the past. Our current social tensions often lead us toward maintaining equilibrium within our societies, for example, rather than toward creating more progressive or new social orders. Only by considering the past, present, and future can we orient our actions to bring about substantial constructive changes.

Referring to the past, present, and future is also necessary to maintain orientations to actions and commitments that increase social intelligence. Collective orientations and collective actions—which coordinate the past, present, and future— expedite our efforts to increase social justice, so that we can bring about more lasting constructive changes in our societies.

Beliefs and Values

When we are aware that it is our beliefs that orient our actions, we see that they have powerful impacts on our futures, especially when they connect us directly with particular social values. Because our cultures permeate our day-to-day existence, our values are expressed in everything we do. This means that when we decide to change particular social conditions, we are most effective when we deliberately nurture beliefs that make meaningful connections with our most cherished social values. For example, if we want to orient our actions toward achieving more egalitarian relationships in society, we need to choose beliefs that connect us most directly to values shared by others who are trying to increase egalitarianism.

Some of the most powerful social values which magnify our orientations to our beliefs and actions are equality, inclusiveness, diversity, cooperation, and openness. These values help us to transform our societies into less competitive arenas, with fewer hierarchical ways to get things done. When we orient our actions toward achieving equality, for example, we set the scene for increasing cooperation and openness in our exchanges, so that the quality of relationships in our societies is improved rather than threatened by fight or flight tendencies. When we learn different ways to relate to each other, we orient more of our actions toward achieving cooperative goals and open discourse.

Our beliefs necessarily encourage, or even generate, particular values and actions. In these respects our beliefs are catalysts which allow us to design constructive strategies to deal with our inevitable social problems. When we deliberately use particular beliefs to orient our actions, we are more likely to make meaningful connections to specific values.

Our values reflect our understanding of social realities. If we choose to use or emphasize values that are different from the mainstream values of our society, we should single out and articulate which values we aim for, in order to persuade others to see some of the same social realities. Once we have a vision of possibilities for the future, we use our different values to guide us in reconstructing our current social realities, so that we build better communities and societies more effectively. Whether or not we choose to emphasize the values of inclusiveness, diversity, or pluralism, for example, we build what we trust will be preferred social conditions for a better tomorrow, due to the impacts our values have on our orientations and actions.

Social intelligence helps us to sort out our many options to orient our actions according to our beliefs and values, or according to the visions we construct from our beliefs and values. Our social intelligence teaches us to size up our social situations by paying attention to social facts. This shows us that inevitably some beliefs, actions, orientations, or visions work better than others. In the spirit of the essential pragmatism of social intelligence, we are often persuaded to follow what appears to be the most effective route to achieve our valued goals. Social intelligence enables us to act with positive results, because we realize that making responsible choices ultimately enables us to increase social justice.

As well as considering particular social values, we learn to value different aspects of our everyday lives. For example, we value social intelligence, and place a high priority on increasing our social intelligence, regardless of the discipline required and the difficulties involved in cultivating and applying social intelligence. We also value ourselves, so that we are less likely to fall prey to others' exploitations, or less likely to become discouraged when we inevitably make mistakes in our trial and error ways of doing things. In addition, we value social facts which suggest directions for us to take; we value specific purposes that guide our explorations of social realities; and we value meanings that make our day-to-day lives richer and fulfilling.

Having beliefs which connect us to these values increases our capacities to live fully. We orient our lives deliberately, in order to make our beliefs and values deeper and broader, and in order to have more control over the consequences of our actions. As a result, we are surer that we lead our own lives, rather than exist vicariously. Social intelligence answers existential issues and concerns, by clarifying our orientations, purposes, and directions.

Focus

Being aware of social influences in historical contexts helps us to focus on what is most significant in the present and future.

For example, when we understand more about the evolution of families in different societies, we see patterns in continuities that have existed to the present, and appreciate more fully the power and complexity of how families continue to meet individual and social needs. Because families are the most universal social institution, examining them enables us to understand the intensity of the needs generated by human dependence in our survival, as well as what might make us extinct.

Families meet our life cycle needs, as well as our personal needs for intimacy. Even though families are often weakened by the reduced power of traditions, they are not easily eliminated. Because alternatives to families have not yet been able to meet family or group needs for extended periods of time, it is extremely difficult to change some of the established repetitions of behavior in our family interactions. Our beliefs about families are conditioned by these continuities in social structures and social needs, so that both our families and our beliefs about families resist change.

It is only when we focus on what we really want our families to do—for example, to look toward the future rather than to be totally immersed in the past or present—that we gain clear perspectives on what we think our family beliefs should be. In order to bring about at least some of these changes, we need to orient our behavior according to beliefs that lead us in these constructive directions. This task takes considerable resolve and commitment, due to families' resistance to making changes. If we manage to sustain our focus on these ideals and goals, however, our beliefs will move us toward a future that will endure, as well as inspire continued constructive adaptations in difficult modern conditions.

Similarly, when we explore the evolution of religions in different cultures or societies, we can identify the conservative forces of religions and religious values. We appreciate more fully how secularization and modernization have challenged traditional religious practices and beliefs, for example, and how important it may still be to use religions as guides to our beliefs, thinking, and behavior. We also need to imagine how particular modifications of religious beliefs—for example, beliefs in social justice—can enliven our religious and social practices in today's and tomorrow's worlds.

Understanding historical contexts of religions sharpens our awareness of the stakes of holding particular religious beliefs, and gives us more choices for orienting our behavior through our religious beliefs. Being able to use religious beliefs as motivations and orientations strengthens the impacts of our actions. Much of our increased clarity about these matters is achieved by continuing to focus on the social sources of our religious beliefs and our religious goals. Even if focusing on our religious beliefs merely shows us contrasts between our traditional religious concerns and our newfound interests in applying social intelligence through increasing social justice, this perspective enables us to make more deliberate choices of beliefs as orientations to our actions.

When we focus on the histories of our social classes, as well as on our social class beliefs, we gain control over important social class dynamics in our present and future decision-making. When we have assessed the significance of our social class biases in our views of self and the world, we change our beliefs, so that they serve us better as orientations for our actions in accomplishing goals which reflect the common good and social justice. For example, we orient our actions by focusing on increasing opportunities for all in our societies, and by giving our attention to beliefs and actions which encourage new ways to organize people, or new ways to embrace diversity and inclusiveness.

It is relatively easy to let our cultures develop as they may, without exploring their historical roots or current impacts. However, when we understand important aspects of cultural changes, such as how industrialization broke through established traditions and customs, or how modern materialistic cultures emphasize consumer goods and services, we begin to exercise control over our cultural choices. Because distinctive modern cultures appeared only relatively recently, many of our current cultural beliefs are based on new conditions rather than those of the past. By contrast, deliberately focusing on broad time perspectives allows us to be more open to making changes in our cultural beliefs, so that we nurture new cultural priorities, or more idealistic cultural goals, as orientations to our actions.

Because cultural beliefs are often tied to special interests—for example, they may be more closely related to mainstream cultures than to specific group cultures—we must be cautious in our assessments of cultural trends. Furthermore, social intelligence suggests that it is more productive and more constructive to focus on orientations that embrace cooperative cultural inclusiveness and diversity, rather than coercive mainstream values and beliefs.

We also need to focus on our societal beliefs, and the social origins of our societal beliefs, in order to clarify our orientations to actions. We tend to take broad social influences for granted, without questioning them, in most everyday situations. However, social intelligence shows us that when we are more discriminating about accepting societal beliefs as our own, we see new options and new opportunities to make the world a better place more clearly. Having sufficient social intelligence to undertake these tasks depends on our capacities to see and focus on societal beliefs for what they are, as well as to find the courage to change them, when needed, as orientations to our actions.

Facts

We increase our social intelligence when we continually check the results of our actions with the social facts of our particular situations. This does not mean that we halt our quests to increase our social intelligence, especially if we do not receive immediate constructive tangible results after we have acted, but rather that we should be wary of proceeding in directions that seem unproductive, where repetitions of facts confirm that problematic social conditions remain unchanged.

When we concentrate on selecting beliefs to motivate us and orient our actions, we need to be guided by the facts of our situations, in order to better choose our beliefs, or in order to reinforce our choices of beliefs. Where evidence points to the ineffectiveness of our beliefs as motivations, or as orientations to our actions, we need to replace those beliefs that do not work for us. If this happens, turning toward particular social values—such as peace or freedom, for example—will suggest wider ranges of beliefs, so that we choose other beliefs as catalysts to increase the effectiveness of our actions.

Being socially intelligent requires that we use facts to choose and nurture our beliefs. Applying social intelligence principles also requires that we check our progress toward increasing our social intelligence, through examining as many of the facts of our situations as possible. Fact-finding and fact-checking are central to our understanding and applications of social intelligence, because this is how we face and deal with realities, without getting unnecessarily diverted by our ideals, rhetoric, or day-dreams.

Facts help us to be objective about ourselves, our beliefs, our motives, our orientations, and our actions. Unless we can honestly assess the pros and cons of facts related to our situations and our societies, we are inevitably pushed and pulled by powerful social influences. Facts provide ways to ground or center our actions, so that we not only view our lives more objectively, but also act more freely to avoid the coerciveness of unwanted social influences.

When we do not know how to collect social facts, we may appreciate some of the differences that facts make by collecting facts about our family histories or local histories. Connecting family and local histories to national and international histories provides us with living social contexts, and makes our starting points in understanding social influences more secure. We place current events or present personal crises in broader social contexts, for example, in order to understand their connections to social influences and social issues. These strategies make broad social trends integral parts of current events in present crises. In addition, examining the histories of social problems and social issues is an effective way to identify and generate related social facts.

The questions we need to ask, in assembling social facts, revolve around "how," "where," and "what," rather than "why." "Why" prompts more theological or philosophical lines of questioning than "how," "where," or "what," which lead us more directly to collect facts. The questions of "how," "where," and "what" also help us to be more critical about our choices in beliefs, as well as more focused in our orientations to action. Questioning is one of the most significant ways in which we increase our social intelligence. We question the usefulness of our beliefs, the constructiveness of our actions, and the effectiveness of our ideals, to make trial and error assessments of our intentions and their results. Facts are our prisms for amassing and interpreting this information.

Taking charge of our beliefs helps us to use our chosen beliefs to motivate our actions. Refining our orientations to our actions, with respect to our beliefs, sharpens our perceptions of our goals and ideals, as well as our awareness of our successes in attaining our goals, or in approaching our ideals. In the final analysis it is our actions that bring about our individual and collective goals.

When we try to understand our personal situations as being individually created, we miss the mark. We must connect the facts of our personal situations to broader social networks or contexts, in order to be more objective and more accurate in our assessments. When the facts we link to our personal situations span local, national, and international contexts, we know that we have delved as deeply as possible into social intelligence principles. Although we should not necessarily discard abstract ideals or religious perspectives, at the same time we need to retain ways of checking our beliefs with facts if the world is to become a better place, and if we are to be both individually and socially fulfilled.

IX. Actions Change Beliefs

B eliefs change actions, and actions change beliefs. Because our actions flow from the deepest parts of ourselves— including layers of beliefs we do not recognize or acknowledge—we gain autonomy and independence by identifying the social sources of as many of our actions and beliefs as we can, and by making more objective choices about which beliefs we want to make our own. We also discover more about our beliefs, when we observe our actions and their consequences in relation to our understanding, being, social connections, and world views.

Our motivations and orientations to our actions are significant influences on what we do, and on how much we accomplish, whether we are aware of what our motivations and orientations are or not. Ideally, we not only know what our motivating and orienting beliefs are, but we also continue to deliberately select our preferred beliefs to serve as motivations and orientations to our actions. When we do not have sufficient reliable information or knowledge about our beliefs, we may choose to act expressly for the purpose of revealing and discovering what our beliefs are.

If we plunge into acting, without any forethought about our beliefs, we can still look at our responses to our own actions, so that we can find the power of our beliefs from our actual behavior. For example, we may ask ourselves what the purposes of our actions were, or how we can transform our intentions into motives and orientations for future actions. We may also examine what the meanings and directions of our actions were, which priorities were implied by our actions, and what we accomplished through our actions.

Scrutinizing our actions, rather than our beliefs, in order to understand connections between our beliefs and actions, frees us from being stuck in ruts or having limitations. Our breakthroughs in these situations occur when we gain a deeper awareness about what our beliefs really are, so that we gradually learn how to use our preferred beliefs as motivations and orientations for working toward more clearly specified goals.

We often consider our spontaneous actions as being largely independent of our beliefs, motivations, and orientations. However, when we use principles of social intelligence to understand our beliefs over sufficiently long periods of time, we appreciate how all of our motivations, orientations, and actions are necessarily rooted in our beliefs in some way. We realize the different degrees of spontaneity in our actions, and come to see that our actions—however spontaneous they may appear to be—are consistently linked to our deepest beliefs, whether we like this fact or not.

Becoming socially intelligent ultimately involves a life-time review, critique, and selection of our most meaningful beliefs and priorities. We are not static in our understanding or our actions, and our interests in becoming socially intelligent move us to explore, examine, and negotiate our beliefs on a continuing basis. Given these complex processes of increasing our social intelligence, we should not hesitate to act promptly when needed, so that we can reflect about and assess our actions later. Understanding our beliefs, motivations, and orientations does not impede our spontaneous or planned actions, but rather becomes a goal to be accomplished in the long run.

Our actions are catalysts that have the power to transform our beliefs. For example, personal, national, or international crises frequently provoke our actions, reactions, and passions. In these critical situations we need to reassess our beliefs, and to remain open to developing and accepting new beliefs. Losses or unexpected tragedies require us to deal directly with our immediate situations, as well as to reevaluate our social conditions, ourselves, and our beliefs, in order to make successful adaptations to our changed circumstances. For example, we redefine our beliefs so that they carry us forward, and we refine our orientations to life so that they are more realistic.

Our actions reinforce our goals and commitments as historical actors, and show us how to make more responsible choices. We learn as much as we can from our actions, to ensure that our beliefs work for us. Past, present, and future impacts of our actions also yield important information about our beliefs, which makes us more aware and vigilant about how much we depend on our beliefs as we go about our daily business.

Because our actions necessarily reflect our values, they show us how to reformulate our beliefs when necessary. For example, when we focus on the values and facts expressed by our actions, we control our actions and beliefs to some extent, and we eventually become more effective historical actors.

Becoming an Historical Actor

Even though we are all historical actors—everything we do has societal dimensions and impacts our societies—social intelligence shows us that we make more effective contributions when we are aware of our actions, especially of the links between our actions and our beliefs. However, there are inevitable crises or stressful situations whenever we go along with the current social momentum; take independent stands in order to survive; actively resist the social momentum; or act with spontaneity rather than forethought. Because our spontaneous actions or reactions instantly plunge us into maelstroms of social influences, social intelligence assures us that we will resurface from these powerful forces resourcefully, especially when we realize that we can be enlightened historical actors in the long run.

The more we assume responsibilities, as historical actors, for our own critiques and deliberations about our beliefs and values, the more likely it is that we will take socially intelligent action under pressure. When we act or react in stressful circumstances, we initially think that our actions are totally spontaneous, rather than considered. However, we discover later that we had developed trustworthy habits in applying social intelligence to our actions in most circumstances. Social intelligence predisposes us to act constructively rather than destructively, due to our awareness of the motivations and orientations of our actions.

Similarly, we develop constructive habits in linking our deeper understanding of the past, present, and future to our actions, and carry this awareness forward in whatever we do as historical actors. Furthermore, when we examine the consequences of our actions, we sometimes see that what we do in pressured circumstances can be more enlightened, or more constructive, than actions taken after careful deliberation.

When we live according to principles of social intelligence, we gradually become responsible historical actors in spite of ourselves. We mature by changing our beliefs or changing our actions, so that our daily routines express our fuller awareness of the power of social influences. These consequences reinforce our inclinations and commitments to be historical actors.

Deepening our commitments to live according to social intelligence principles consolidates our actions, reinforces our goals to increase social intelligence and social justice, and reassures us. Our actions show us that the challenging tasks of becoming socially intelligent and of becoming historical actors are not easily reversed by changing circumstances. When we become who we are, through applying social intelligence principles, we gain some degree of protection from others' pressures and our own whims.

Becoming an historical actor is an important goal or objective of increasing our social intelligence. Our concerns must ultimately be directed to our actions, rather than to endless critical thinking or deliberations about our beliefs, because we need to act in order to be socially intelligent. Although we have much to learn, experiencing the tangible rewards and meaningful fulfillment of applying social intelligence to our lives inspires us. For example, once we develop missions as historical actors, we find that this increases our senses of agency, our actions reinforce or change our beliefs, and our actions increasingly produce our most desired consequences.

As historical actors, we gain confidence in the power of our responsible actions and their effective results. We learn, through our actions, that our beliefs continue to be very significant, and that we strengthen our beliefs through the efficacy and power of our actions. Thus our empowerment as historical actors is supported by both our beliefs and our actions. When we are more socially intelligent, we place higher priorities on our actions rather than on further analyses of our beliefs, even though we must necessarily stay open to new views, new options, and social facts. Ultimately, when we have satisfactorily assessed the social origins and social impacts of our beliefs and actions, we can live fully and achieve our well-intentioned goals.

Understanding the power of our actions makes us appreciate how our actions generate facts that test our beliefs. We are freer to test our beliefs through our actions, and being an historical actor makes us increasingly active and aware in varied social settings. Actions, as well as beliefs about taking action, permeate more of our being, doing, and historical contributions than before, especially as we build on the past in the present, to create more viable futures.

Responsible Choices

We know our choices are responsible when we can predict, with some degree of accuracy, what their action consequences will be. Our actions are acid tests of the effectiveness of our beliefs, motivations, and orientations, and their constructiveness shows whether or not we made responsible choices among our beliefs.

When our actions show that our beliefs were either ineffective in their impacts on our actions, or led to inappropriate choices, our responsibilities lie in finding alternative beliefs, examining their social origins, and substituting new beliefs for our former beliefs. Formulating critical assessments of our beliefs and their action consequences are vital aspects of being responsible, and they ultimately increase our social intelligence.

When we use social intelligence to guide our choices in beliefs and our decisions to act, we examine the extent to which our beliefs reflect our awareness and knowledge of families, religions, social classes, cultures, and societies. Because we build our social intelligence on understanding the importance of these crucial influences on the social realities of our situations, we need to keep these perspectives in mind. Otherwise, they become dangerous fault lines in the foundations of our thinking and actions.

Focusing on the breadth and scope of our beliefs and actions in our families, religions, social classes, cultures, and societies makes us more responsible in our choices of beliefs and actions. When we know that we have paid sufficient attention to these significant aspects of our lives, we find that we are less vulnerable to assaults by our emotions, by others' emotions or power, and by destructive social influences.

Our choices of beliefs and actions are eventually more responsible when we communicate our socially intelligent strategies to others. For example, when we raise children—or influence grandchildren—to be aware of the power and complexity of their families, beliefs, social classes, cultures, and societies, they become more independent and more effective in what they accomplish. Consequently, they are more able to create and follow dreams that make a difference to themselves and others.

However, our responsible choices do not lie solely in relation to the younger members of our families. We should also address as many broad human or social needs as possible, so that we can pass on information about social intelligence or social justice to those who are interested and ready to hear it, as well as willing to put it into action. These responsible actions increase constructive communications about social intelligence and social justice, and bring us closer to achieving social justice ideals collectively. Our shared socially intelligent perspectives also make us more able to embrace needs and responsibilities related to global conditions, so that we can make a difference on a broader scale, as well as in our local or home territories.

When we make responsible choices to teach social intelligence to other people directly and indirectly, we aim to make them more independent in their specific uses and applications of social intelligence principles. We do not merely help others by doing tasks for them that bring immediate tangible benefits, but rather we get engaged in educating them about how social intelligence can enlighten their own actions. Our responsible aims suggest pathways that dependably inspire others' constructive actions, so that they also ultimately increase social justice.

These goals are difficult to achieve in responsible ways. It is much easier to direct people about what we think should be done in particular situations, than it is to suggest how they might accomplish their own goals with social intelligence. To the extent that we explain social intelligence, or the practical significance of social justice, only when asked, we are more socially intelligent about sharing our knowledge with others. By contrast, doing others' tasks directly for them often turns out to be an escape, a feel-good enterprise, a retreat, or a roundabout, inferior way to support others.

As our time and energies are necessarily limited, we must allocate them judiciously. For example, we need to be cautious in undertaking new projects, as well as sure that our new ventures are both socially intelligent and oriented to social justice. Consequently, establishing priorities according to these criteria requires us to formulate beliefs and actions that uphold the values of increasing social intelligence and social justice.

Another important aspect of responsible choices is that we need to act collectively as much as possible, so that we increase our effectiveness in bringing about our shared goals. When we act collectively, rather individually, our decisions are enlightened from a wide variety of social sources. Working cooperatively to achieve shared goals increases the impacts of our collective social intelligence, and strengthens the outcomes of our actions. Our collective actions change our individual and social beliefs, and increase probabilities that societies participate more imaginatively and more constructively in globalization. We predictably benefit from acting in these directions, because they increase our collective social intelligence, and our collective capacities to work toward increasing the common good and social justice.

Past, Present, and Future

Social intelligence encourages us to become more objective about our pasts, present, and futures. In order to understand the broad, social contexts of our situations, we necessarily take a step back from our usual everyday pressures, so that we see and assess a wide spectrum of social influences. Being more objective allows us to focus more effectively on social facts related to changes in our pasts, present, and futures, so that we understand the beliefs, motives, and orientations expressed by our actions more fully.

158

IX. Actions Change Beliefs

When we examine our actions in contexts of the past, present, and future, we discover that the individuals we thought we were are not necessarily factual or realistic assessments of who we are. The frequencies of our actions in particular spheres, such as listening to music, may reveal that more of our commitments and energies are directed to these activities than we realized. Our new action-based views of ourselves help us to discover that we may be more passive than active, in relation to existing social pressures, and that we can benefit from changing these imbalances in our attention, energies, and intentions.

When we identify increased numbers of facts about our actions in our pasts, present, and futures, we can use our past, present and future actions as inspirations for change. Facts are not only important to explain our actions, but they are also clear markers of what our priorities and possibilities are. Because correlations between facts and actions are direct and intractable, patterns in facts reflect patterns in actions, which often have the power to change our beliefs. Thus assessments of our facts and actions motivate us to make changes where needed.

Checking facts about our actions in our pasts, present, and futures makes us more critical, as well as better informed, about how we act. Even though facts about our pasts and present do not determine our future actions, they often clarify our underlying beliefs about our actions and options. Being critical about our actions, especially as we assess our odds for repeating our actions of the past and present in the future, sharpens our awareness of the necessity to make choices and decisions about our priorities. Understanding our past and present actions more fully, for example, empowers us to take stands which curb those actions that are the most destructive to ourselves and others.

When we look toward the future, it is sometimes not so much our actions that predispose us to repetitions, as it is our beliefs about how often our past actions tend to re-emerge through time. For example, we often accept the belief that our pasts impact our present and futures, before our pasts are actually directly linked to our present and futures through our actions. Although our actions may change our beliefs, our beliefs about our actions in our pasts and present also strongly influence the extent to which our pasts and present are ultimately connected to our futures through our actions.

Our attitudes to actions in our pasts, present, and futures also influence how we become historical actors, as well as whether or not we are effective historical actors. In order to sustain actions which are well-coordinated in past, present, and future contexts, we must continue to be objective and critical about our actions, so that we can behave judiciously at all times.

Our choices in beliefs about our actions are more responsible when we consider different time perspectives. When we believe that our actions in the present change our beliefs about the future, for example, they are more likely to do so. Specifying which of our beliefs about time-related actions in our families, religions, social classes, cultures, and societies promote or block changes we want to make, is an effective way to assess these influences. Furthermore, when social intelligence guides our assessments, our actions are more likely to establish constructive futures, which increase the common good and social justice.

Ultimately, our actions—rather than our beliefs about our actions—yield sustained direction, meaning, and purpose in individual and social changes. Examining our past and present actions helps us to connect our beliefs with values more directly and more meaningfully, for example. As we grew to maturity, did our actions show that we changed or accepted our parents' values? How do our current actions influence our present and future beliefs and values? Do our present actions increase our social intelligence, so that we contribute more to the common good and social justice now and in the future? Do our current actions show us what beliefs we need to enlighten our present and future?

One of the most powerful arguments for linking the past, present, and future in our actions is our limited lifespan. When we realize that our resources of time and energy are limited, we are more able to step back from the past and present, in order to assess what our most meaningful action priorities are for our futures. Also, knowing that we have limited options increases our willingness to make better futures for ourselves and others. For example, if our futures seem nearer to us than much of the past, we are often more willing to work with others to increase our effectiveness in the present for the future.

Beliefs in existential necessities to take actions to better ourselves encourage us to focus on accomplishing our goals, and keep us open to facts which motivate and orient our actions. We are renewed through changing our beliefs and actions, and through continuing to refine our beliefs and actions, which consequently increases the common good and social justice.

Beliefs and Values

Because actions influence our beliefs, whether we realize this or not, we gradually embrace broader social values as we continue to act and formulate our beliefs according to social intelligence principles. Thus our beliefs necessarily express particular values through our actions.

However, when we examine our beliefs more closely than our actions, we see that whatever we find meaningful in our cultures and societies is a unique version of some general trends in beliefs or values in our societies. In these respects we are creatures of our cultures, because there is considerable overlap between individuals' beliefs, social values, and societal cultures.

Social intelligence allows us to see the deep influences of beliefs and values in our everyday situations. One of the major reasons why beliefs and values have such a strong and lasting impact on how we think, and what we do, is that they influence us at emotional levels of our being and awareness. For example, how we see ourselves and our worlds is imbued with a wide range of strong emotions, which often makes it extremely difficult to change our beliefs and values.

In some cases our beliefs contrast with mainstream values. Our increased awareness, from social intelligence, helps us to assess the extent to which we want, or do not want, to invest ourselves in beliefs which are not as clearly or as directly connected to values in the wider society. We may put ourselves at a disadvantage, for example, when we do not speak the same language of values as other people, especially as some individuals and groups have strong emotional investments against accepting contrasting or conflicting beliefs and values.

Thus our beliefs motivate and orient our actions, and tend to either reinforce or challenge their related values. Because social intelligence shows us that collective actions are particularly effective, we try to work more deliberately with other people to accomplish our goals. This may mean that we sacrifice some of the idiosyncratic aspects of our beliefs, so that we can connect more directly with widely-held values in society at large, and benefit from being integral parts of a collective consciousness or collective actions.

Because our values are directly related to social ideals, we may find that using ideals as goals—for example, when we pursue social justice—helps us to transcend some of the inevitable frustrations, difficulties, and hurdles involved in our everyday negotiations with others. When we are aware of the values and ideals implied by our beliefs, we weather obstacles more easily, and approach our endeavors with greater perseverance. Seeing the broader meanings of our beliefs also moves us into spheres of values and ideals, which are often shared by large proportions of our populations. Refining our beliefs, values, and ideals launches our actions into wide social arenas. When we connect our beliefs with global values, for example, we become more active participants in global processes, sometimes in concert with large numbers of people. Clarifying our values strengthens these associations and commitments, so that we are more effective in impacting both national and international spheres. Joining global social movements, or international community organizations, are examples of how our outreach is increased and strengthened by orienting our beliefs and actions toward broad purposes and widespread values.

Synchronizing our beliefs, motives, orientations, and ideals successfully depends on our social intelligence. When we deliberately revise and substitute our beliefs, so that they make more sense in relation to our goals, our actions are better integrated and effective. We need to create visions of what an increased common good looks like, or of how particular aspects of social justice can be brought into being, in order to make constructive differences. For example, when we see where we want to go, we connect our efforts to social values more easily and more productively.

Sometimes we choose to cultivate one particular social value as exclusively as possible—such as freedom—rather than clusters of related values or different values. Although narrow goals have historically been used by zealots, they can also usefully orient us toward maintaining a healthy single-mindedness for accomplishing our most cherished goals. Having clarity in our most significant beliefs and values simplifies our day-to-day decisions, so that we stay on track and accomplish more of what we intend.

Focus

In order to apply social intelligence principles on a daily basis, we need to be alert to as many of the social influences around us as possible. Our social conditioning and cultural ways of doing things accompany us everywhere, so that even when we deliberately choose to act automatically, we are vulnerable to some degree of takeover by our social systems' needs.

For example, our social institutions of families, religions, the economy, education, and politics maintain equilibrium in societies, and make it possible for societies—rather than individuals—to survive. Consequently, we easily become pawns of broad social influences, such as social classes, that are driven by power relations, rather than by individual or social needs to preserve individual and social freedoms.

Maintaining a focus on broad social complexities appears to be a paradox or impossible. Customarily we narrow our focuses, in order to sustain them over long periods of time, which excludes extraneous concerns and sharpens our attention. However, being socially intelligent requires that we essentially open eyes at the backs of our heads and at our sides, as well as in front of us, so that we are truly watchful and objective about whatever goes on around us.

Being socially intelligent requires that we maintain a broad field of clear vision, as well as give attention to particular tasks that only we can perform, due to our knowledge of the social influences that affect us the most. We need to stay connected to historical changes, for example, by pursuing tasks in the present with concerns for the future. When we develop these habits of focus and observation, we are more able to be socially intelligent in our responses to current conditions and pressures.

Another way to focus is to pay attention to how our actions changed our beliefs in the past. When we examine earlier stages of our lives, for example, we see more clearly that some of our major turning points involved our actions, rather than shifts in our beliefs. Tracing these connections shows us that our actions made considerable differences to how we saw things during or after important events.

For example, attending school for the first time, meeting relatives who had lost contact with our families, making lasting friendships, traveling abroad, living away from home, earning degrees, marrying, having children, becoming grandparents, and caring for elderly parents are ways in which our actions often shocked our belief systems, and changed our beliefs, because we pursued different strategies due to the stresses of our new social or cultural encounters. Moreover, we eventually adapted to these life-changing situations through acknowledging and modifying our former beliefs about self, others, groups, societies, and the world.

We can also focus on our actions and day-to-day behavior through tracking the extent to which we follow our own goals or others' goals. When we understand patterns of interaction in our families, for example, we can identify major social influences in our development as children, adolescents, and adults. During our formative years, we were necessarily beholden to our families' power structures, as well as to pressures from their cultural systems. When we are adults, however, we need to determine the extent to which we were coerced to conform to our families' dominant religious practices, for example, and to identify who led our families in their religious observances.

Understanding our families through such focuses allows us to see how we were, and still are, caught up in our most emotional family dependencies. Defining who we are, and what we want to do, is necessarily a lifetime effort, which can be guided and supported by increasing our social intelligence. When we predict more accurately how family emotions and social pressures operate in our families, and in other social settings, we can distinguish being in control of our abilities to act responsibly, from being pushed or pulled to accommodate to others' directives or expectations.

We become more independent through social intelligence when we focus on the impacts our families, social situations, and individual intentions have on how we act. When we see who we are in relation to our families, beliefs, social classes, cultures, and societies, we assess our experiences of freedom and autonomy more accurately, especially when we scrutinize facts underlying our behavior. For example, focusing on the impacts of dominant social influences, which largely define our particular situations, helps us to disentangle ourselves from others.

Maintaining such a meaningful focus shows us how to act with social intelligence. However, we also gain by moving our focuses among different perspectives, in order to respond effectively to our changing circumstances. Although using any one focus is valuable, keeping only one focus ultimately restricts our vision and rigidifies our beliefs. We maintain flexibility in our focuses, so that we can focus both within and among the different major social influences in our lives. Moving our focuses helps us to refine and confirm the choices we make, and considering different focuses clarifies our social circumstances, as well as our actions and the particular tasks we want to accomplish.

Facts

If we are in doubt as to what the facts of our lives are, it is useful to consider the most important events in our lives, and our most frequent activities. We ask such questions as what it is that we have done that is most memorable? What do we continue to do that is meaningful and significant for us, and for what we want to accomplish? The facts of our lives are closely associated with our actions, and we strengthen our senses of agency and control over our actions when we consider sufficient facts about our past and current situations.

Our ages, household compositions, assets, occupations, family structures, locations of our homes, education, family backgrounds, nationalities, travel habits, friendships, religions, religious upbringing, and likes or dislikes are among those facts which describe, and to a certain extent explain, who we are. Social intelligence provides views of the social influences which affect the facts of our circumstances, and our beliefs reflect and interact with these facts.

If we change our household compositions—which is one fact of our circumstances—our beliefs about self, others, and the world are challenged or modified. In addition, when unexpected major events occur, such as the loss of a relative or a friend, our deepest beliefs are inevitably upset, and we are compelled to reassess, and often change our beliefs, in order to resolve the gap between what we thought was factual reality and our loss. These accommodations ultimately make our lives more meaningful. Social intelligence is a beacon, which sheds light on how we should build whatever is most significant and most real to us, as we make such adjustments.

Looking at the facts of expected or unexpected changes in our lives helps us to focus on our actions, and to see both our beliefs and our actions as expressions of important parts of ourselves. Even though our beliefs are human and social creations, which are ever changing, they provide security because they anchor us in our complex worlds, and play crucial roles in our actions. Similarly, even though we are in constant motion as we go about our daily affairs, our actions anchor our beliefs in facts, or reveal our deepest beliefs to us. This reciprocity between our beliefs and actions keeps us on course to increase our social intelligence, and to work toward social justice.

Another aspect of social intelligence, that helps us to link facts with our beliefs and actions, is its acknowledgement of facts in the complex and powerful social influences of families, beliefs, social classes, cultures, and societies. When we understand and take seriously how these influences affect our circumstances, opportunities, goals, world views, and actions, we come to terms with their facts through becoming more socially intelligent. Seeing the social origins of our beliefs in families, religions, classes, cultures, and societies helps us to link the facts of our situations to our beliefs and actions. We become human by being exposed to interactions in the spheres of families, beliefs, social classes, cultures, and societies, and we become stronger and more fulfilled when we take charge of our beliefs and actions by examining and accepting these facts.

Decision-making is an early stage of taking action. Collecting and scrutinizing facts before we make decisions, increases their thoughtfulness and responsibility. By considering facts, our decisions become more firmly rooted in social realities, for example. Therefore, we seek out the most significant social facts of our situations, whatever these situations are, in order to ensure that we make the wisest decisions possible. Our actions will then guide our beliefs, and lead to formulating clearer beliefs to meet our socially intelligent goals.

In considering what kind of world we want to create for coming generations, we must review past and current facts and actions, as well as ideals like social justice. Facts and actions keep us honest, ground us in social realities, help us to design practical plans, and allow us to make slow but real progress toward social justice. In these ways facts and actions prevent us from being carried away by empty rhetoric, which is ultimately counter-productive. Our social intelligence needs to be built on solid foundations of facts and actions, as well as beliefs, if it is to have lasting constructive effects. Thus facts and actions enlighten our beliefs, just as beliefs enlighten our actions.

What Kind of World?

X. People and Beliefs

People embody their beliefs, and bring them into the world through their actions. When we consider the social origins of our beliefs, we see that our beliefs derive largely from people, and that they have been communicated to us both directly and indirectly by people throughout the years. Sometimes we know the particular significant others who influenced us the most—such as our parents or other close family members—because of our acceptance of many of their beliefs. But often we are not aware of specifically who influenced us in forming our beliefs. For example, many of the cultural sources of our beliefs stay unknown, and we have to acknowledge that faceless crowds have had strong impacts on our beliefs and values.

However hard we try to uncover the social origins of our beliefs, we accept many beliefs that seem rootless, but which also wield considerable power over our decision-making. In principle, these beliefs also have social origins, which we may discover later, especially if we conduct our daily business by using social intelligence, or if we continue to increase our social intelligence. All we need to concern ourselves with in the present is moving in directions of social intelligence and social justice, and being alert to possibilities of finding more of the social origins of our beliefs, particularly those embodied by specific individuals or groups.

Social intelligence provides us with new ideas about the nature of human nature, including the roles played by our beliefs and the social origins of our beliefs. Our human interdependence suggests that we are strongly influenced by others' beliefs about self, people, groups, society, and the world, as well as by our own beliefs. Some of the beliefs which consistently affect us the most are our beliefs about the social spheres of families, religions, social classes, cultures, and societies, which are important building blocks of self, motives, orientations, and values. Our social intelligence, characters, and actions develop from our beliefs about these social influences and their effects.

Sometimes people embody particular traditions through their beliefs. As children we were often comforted by the sound and feel of certain traditions, for example, which were often difficult to break or modify later. These traditions frequently became our adult habits of thought and action, even though we were by now both mature and well-educated.

Social intelligence gives us access to these influential traditional beliefs, and provides ways to assess how we practice them. Ultimately we must choose either to stay committed to our traditional beliefs, or to challenge and question them in light of the facts of our present situations.

It is useful to trace our traditional beliefs to particular individuals or groups, because this makes us more able to assess them for what they are, as well as sufficiently objective to decide whether or not to perpetuate our loyalty to them. Through these means, social intelligence gives us new ways to look at our lives, new ideas to consider, and new directions to take on a daily basis.

Because social intelligence encourages us to live according to principles of social justice, social justice can also be used as a means to assess whether we want to foster specific social traditions through our actions. When we examine the consequences of our actions, for example, we may see that they do not increase the common good or further social justice. Ideally this awareness makes us change some of our beliefs and priorities, so that we embrace our relatively new value of social justice more fully.

Social intelligence shows us that it is important to face the future with questions rather than answers, so that we can innovate and design new ways to approach old problems. Understanding people as fully as possible is vital to this enterprise. We need not only to look at our pasts and present with the deeper understanding of social intelligence, but also to move toward the future with socially intelligent goals and principles of social justice. For example, unless we design innovative ways to deal with the emotional aspects of our social being, we may implode or explode in our efforts to survive.

When we are aware historical actors, we orient our actions with a distinctive breadth of vision which is based on social intelligence, and on our knowledge of peoples' individual and social needs. By contrast, goals and plans which are founded on mistaken assumptions about human nature and social influences are doomed to fail. We must scrutinize the social implications of our innate interdependence, which all too often increases our tendencies to react negatively to others, rather than to work peacefully and cooperatively. Only socially intelligent assessments of human nature allow us to carry the day with visions and plans that have constructive consequences, because these meet real human, individual, and social needs.

Families

The most significant social sources of our beliefs, according to social intelligence, are our families. This is partly because our nuclear families and extended kin groups are critical players when we absorb others' beliefs in the earliest stages of our development. Furthermore, we frequently continue to use many aspects of these initial views of ourselves, others, societies, and the world throughout our lifetimes. Consequently, these innermost core beliefs need to be examined and changed where necessary.

The most practical way to trace the precise sources of beliefs which originate in our families is to consider our relationships and communications with different family members, especially with those who oriented us to life. We need to consider, for example, what were, and perhaps still are, the dominant beliefs which motivated and oriented our parents, siblings, grandparents, cousins, and other relatives. How did we internalize the beliefs we received from our families? To what extent did our most significant family members pass on their own beliefs while teaching us about gender, religion, education, finances, or politics? Who were our families' leaders during the years when we were initially oriented to ourselves, others, and the world?

Social intelligence requires us to ponder who taught us what about human nature, as well as the world, and who gave us compelling examples of this knowledge through their behavior. What did we learn about relationships from our families, for example, or about achieving goals? Who opened up our worlds, so that we could embrace the strange and unknown in society, as well as the familiar? What were the most significant lessons about social realities that we learned from our parents? Did we learn from our parents through what they told us, or through what they did? There are many different angles that we can explore, in order to understand more about how we accepted particular family beliefs as our own.

If is often the beliefs of our most dominant family members that are the most firmly entrenched in our being. Because family dominance usually results from the emotional control or emotional manipulation of our relatives, we must unlearn at least some of the in-depth effects of these experiences, if we want to cultivate our own beliefs now. This move toward becoming more socially intelligent necessarily involves changing our relationships with our dominant family members, so that we come to terms with our own real beliefs. Assessing the social origins of our beliefs includes examining the broad social perspectives of our closest family members, as well as understanding the power of the family emotional influences that may need to be changed.

For example, our grandparents, even when deceased, may continue to be significant sources of our current beliefs. Grandparents deepened our understanding of the passage of time when we were young, merely by being there, and their views about society or history may still be important to us. However, because our grandparents' views may be strongly biased in ways that do not fit well with present social realities, we need to assess and perhaps modify these beliefs. The fact that our most significant family members may have died by no means curtails, or even limits, the influences that their beliefs may continue to have on us. Many of us are motivated by completely mismatched family beliefs for a lifetime, unless we become more objective about our beliefs' sources and substance, as well as become willing to change them.

People past and present are the social sources of our beliefs. Our family dependencies reveal important, otherwise inexplicable, aspects of why we have the beliefs we have. Furthermore, sibling rivalries—or rivalries between cousins— may continue to distort our present priorities, unless we change patterns that were established in the past. In fact, many of the biases and prejudices in our beliefs reflect or result from imbalances in our family relationships.

For example, our beliefs about gender usually derive from beliefs held by several of the women and men in our families. Gender is inevitably lived in particular ways, and some of our earliest memories are of how we were held to different standards to behave as "good girls" or "good boys." Even though we may not have had direct experiences of gay or lesbian family members, we often heard and observed our family members' rigid or flexible beliefs and attitudes about heterosexuality and homosexuality. These are powerful social influences on the ways in which we formulate our own beliefs about sexuality, sexual orientation, and life satisfaction.

Religions

Just as people in our families are significant sources of our beliefs, including our religious beliefs, members of our religious communities also influenced us in developing our religiosity and religious practices. However, our initial family orientations to particular religions, as well as to religions in general, are usually more powerful than the influences of members of our religious communities, even though close friends or revered religious leaders may have strong impacts on us through our families.

To the extent that many of our religious beliefs result from whatever religious upbringing we had, or did not have, examining ways in which we became religious—or not—helps us to scrutinize the beliefs we have about particular religions, or about religions in general. To the extent that we were raised to be very religious, for example, we need to make sure that this orientation does not include bigotry or dogmatic beliefs, which often vilify those who do not share our religious beliefs and experiences.

In all, our more objective assessments of our religious beliefs, through applying social intelligence, include coming to terms with the religious beliefs of those who influenced us the most, even though we may have decided not to be religious. Social intelligence shows us that understanding the social origins of our beliefs has to include a careful accounting of family members' varied religious beliefs, if only at a distance. For example, our families or distant family members who are clearly not religious may have powerful impacts on our religious beliefs and our beliefs about religions.

One reason for the appeal that religious beliefs have for families is the clusters of values that are supported and reinforced by religions. These values frequently define specific family expectations—such as obedience by children—which have historically and traditionally proved themselves useful or meaningful to parents. Therefore, even though many beliefs and ideas associated with religions are considered to be politically conservative or antiquated, families still frequently use and abuse religions to strengthen their authority and sanctions in disciplining their children to be obedient, or to conform to parental expectations. Consequently, when children feel that their parents and God are on the same side, for example, the penalties for not being obedient may seem too horrific for them to imagine.

The first people to consider, in understanding patterns of religious socialization in our families, include the parent who was responsible for our religious upbringing, as well as those relatives who led family religious observances and religious practices when we were young. These people undoubtedly had powerful impacts on our religious and emotional sensibilities, our resulting religious beliefs, and our beliefs about religions. They necessarily played significant—often hidden—roles in our motivations, orientations, and actions, especially in relation to our religious beliefs.

Another way in which people influenced our religious beliefs is how they linked their religious beliefs to society, world views, actions, and social issues. We are often introduced to secular concerns through our parents' and relatives' religious beliefs, and through the examples of our parents' and relatives' religious and secular practices. When we saw, or still see, close positive connections between our significant others' religious beliefs and their everyday life practices, we are usually more inclined to accept their religious beliefs. When we cannot find connections between our relatives' religious beliefs and their practices, we are more likely to become critical of them or their religions, and often do not follow in their footsteps.

Hearing and understanding religious leaders, or those who conduct meaningful devotional practices, also helped us to formulate our own beliefs about religions and religious practices. We may have been attracted to developing a spiritual life, for example, which was only indirectly influenced by organized religions. Whatever the outcomes of developing our own religious beliefs, we have inevitably been influenced by many individuals and groups along the way. For example, we used others' examples and experiences to build our understanding of the many links between our nascent religious beliefs and our religious or secular practices.

If we want to come to terms with the social influences and power of religions and religious traditions in societies, we also need to consider religions' historical and contemporary social conditions. For example, even though secularization and modernization have introduced new ways of being to mass societies, religions still thrive and continue to have devoted followers. In fact, the relatively recent growth of religious fundamentalism is so strong that it threatens some civilizations, especially those with relatively recent trends in more equalized gender and race relations.

Social intelligence points out that extreme religious beliefs and religious power show us how strong religions and religious beliefs are, as individual and social influences. Therefore, we must recognize, respect, and deal with religious influences, whether we are religious or not.

Social Classes

Sometimes we were shocked into learning about social classes when we were young. As children, we usually accepted social classes without realizing what we were doing. We used social class biases in our interactions with others, without being aware of the power that social classes have over how we think and what we do on a daily basis. We also did not initially, or easily, grasp the significance that social classes had for our parents and adult relatives.

As we grew older, events like inviting friends to visit our families sometimes precipitated considerable negative reactivity from our parents. This often seemed incomprehensible to us. Our parents may have advised us, for example, that it would be better not to be a friend of a person we had invited to our home, describing this person as being different from ourselves. Although such situations were perplexing, and often painful, we usually picked up sufficient meanings from innuendoes of our parents' comments about social classes over the years, that we realized that these tensions expressed deeper meanings and implications of social class differences.

Particular stages of our development to adulthood call into question our parents' and families' responses to economic social classes. For example, our choices of schools, our study habits, our development of opportunities to pursue professional careers, our selections of partners or spouses, and our choices of living quarters, travel, or other significant aspects of our lives are often treated with intense interest—and a marked degree of control—by our parents, because they suggest particular social statuses. In these ways we gradually learn to meet our social class expectations as we become adults, with the result that we often choose partners or spouses who are from similar social classes.

Social intelligence helps us to understand the power and significance of social classes, by requiring us to consider the social origins of our different beliefs about social classes, most particularly which family members taught us about social classes when we were young. In order to free ourselves from some of the negative restrictiveness of our own social classes, we need to understand which social class beliefs we embody in our being, seeing, and doing. We also need to be sufficiently objective, so that we make more real choices now about what we want to do with our lives, regardless of our social class influences.

Social intelligence shows us that social classes do not merely reflect the different amounts of material goods that certain groups have. Additional means of stratifying groups are used in our complex contemporary societies, which also need to be identified, considered, and understood. For example, we have to pay attention to how we and our families create and deal with social classes based on religion, gender, sexual orientation, race, ethnicity, ablebodiedness, and education. We need to understand these additional social classes as fully as possible, if we are to free ourselves from their negative, restrictive effects on our choices, decisions, and actions.

In order to make this daunting task manageable, social intelligence encourages us to consider which of our relatives emphasized the importance of social class differences when we were young, and which were most concerned about our choices of schools or friends. These patterns of family interaction help us to see the specific personal and social sources of our social class awareness more clearly.

Heightening our social class awareness, through seeing how we learned about social classes, ultimately frees us from mindlessly repeating social class behavior through the generations. Furthermore, unless we are aware of the complexity and power of social classes, we are not able to successfully choose or pursue ideals and goals like social justice, which transcend class differences. We need to understand as many of the major social influences in societies as possible, through considering the key players in our lives, in order to be socially intelligent. A people-based approach to learning about ourselves also helps us to recognize that the significant subtleties—in our overlapping social class differences and social class interests—are infinite.

Because social intelligence directs us to work toward increasing our own and others' freedom, we do not assess particular relatives' roles in our social class conditioning negatively. We do not blame our relatives for their social class biases, for example, but rather face the facts of our own social class biases as squarely as possible. We formulate and use more positive or more creative social class beliefs to motivate and orient us to increase the common good and realize social justice.

X. People and Beliefs

If we need courage to accomplish the difficult work of neutralizing our social class biases, we should examine some historical sources of social class differences. Then we see more clearly that many modern societies have largely moved away from caste-like structures of social classes without much social mobility, to more open social classes with considerable social mobility. This real progress has been achieved through many varied individual and social changes, and we can now use our social intelligence to continue the momentum of increased opportunities and increased social justice for greater proportions of our populations.

Cultures

Cultures are other crucial social sources of our beliefs, as well as sources of people who helped us to define and nurture our cultural beliefs. When we consider how we accepted particular beliefs about cultures as our own, we should bear in mind who played dominant roles in teaching us—by words or by example—what cultures mean, and how important they are in orienting us towards ourselves, others, societies, and the world.

People are culture carriers. We transmit values and meanings, as well as beliefs, in how we present ourselves to others, in the decisions we make, and in the actions we take. Because we cannot escape the impacts of cultures on our beliefs, we should examine whatever we know about the social sources of our cultural beliefs, in order to gain some control over the choices we make about our cultural beliefs and values. If, on the other hand, we think about our cultural assumptions as facts, for example, we inevitably resist changing the beliefs we absorbed from others, which then control how we formulate our goals and responsibilities.

We come to understand that the people who connect us to our cultural beliefs are frequently from our families, religions, and social classes. However, because cultures suggest

181

international as well as national or local sources, we also find relatively impersonal social origins of our cultural beliefs. In addition to those significant others who play dominant roles in the formation of our beliefs about cultures, we identify players in the multiculturalism of large cities—or in popular cultures—as additional strong influences in the formation of our broadest cultural beliefs and values.

Secularization and modernization are products of economic, political, and cultural changes. At the same time that the middle classes grew and prospered through capitalism, increased cultural choices became available to more people. Families today are more often units of consumption, for example, than units of production, and many of us routinely refine our tastes for goods which serve our recreational interests rather than our survival needs. For example, because we increasingly express ourselves through our choices in music, mass cultures create alternative, virtual worlds beside the workaday realities that our ancestors experienced.

When we make choices among our contemporary cultural options, we often aim to create different family or cohort cultures. We recognize the younger or older members of our families through their tastes in music, or cultural goods, for example. We build our individual and social identities from broad cultural value choices, which are learned, as well as from cultural styles that accentuate social class, race, or gender contrasts.

Social intelligence requires that we seek out not only those individuals who taught us the most about the cultural beliefs and values we absorbed, but also people who made us aware of the vast array of cultural options available to us. A panoramic view of cultures includes less familiar beliefs and values from foreign and exotic cultures, which impact our world views.

Many people embody the same, or similar, cultural beliefs to our own—family members, peer group intimates, or leaders in national cultures. When we examine the social sources of our cultural beliefs, however, we may find it difficult to locate individual people or groups who influenced us directly. In these respects it is perhaps sufficient to identify people with whom we have cultural affinities, so that we can make meaningful social connections to shared experiences of cultural beliefs and values.

Our cultures are vital sources of individual and social changes. When we modify our cultural beliefs, we open up new worlds for ourselves. By substituting different cultural beliefs for our former cultural beliefs, we gain fresh ideals, establish new priorities, and formulate innovative goals to pursue.

Social intelligence requires that we scrutinize the social sources of our cultural beliefs, precisely so that we can make these changes. Because human beings have capacities to learn and modify their cultural beliefs, they are able to see and act in contexts of broad cultural vistas. Our changed cultural beliefs establish new priorities, so that our everyday lives are gradually transformed.

History shows us patterned sequences in changing power relations; broader, more organized economies; and the continued growth of mass cultures. In these respects, the meanings we find in our cultural beliefs may motivate us to accomplish a great deal. By contrast, when we act from foundations of restricted visions of our cultural possibilities, we cannot as easily increase the common good or social justice.

Because the ideal of social justice is largely a cultural product, we need to build cultures which enable us to act collectively to create opportunities for more people. Although we learn to formulate and hold new cultural beliefs, as well as more valuable ideas, these cultural beliefs need to be sufficiently broad, as well as sufficiently coherent, in order to truly benefit from the most constructive aspects of our cultures and societies.

Societies

Our initial beliefs about societies do not usually come to us directly from people in the large, anonymous populations of our own or others' societies, but rather through our relatives and other significant others who orient us to the world at large. The parental, family, or educational task of teaching children about the world is often taken relatively lightly, in spite of its tremendous importance to the children involved, who may eventually understand society as a hostile place, an arena for accomplishment, or varied opportunities to act responsibly.

Our parents' or relatives' beliefs about society are instrumental in providing us with broad perspectives, and in defining issues about understanding people. Teachers, religious leaders, and older friends also introduce us to the world. Therefore, when scrutinizing our beliefs about societies, we need to acknowledge who communicated information and beliefs about societies to us during our childhoods and adolescence, as well as what this information and beliefs meant. We also need to understand why we continued to retain inaccurate beliefs about societies once we became adults, and how we are harmed by holding on to particular faulty beliefs about societies that do not serve us well.

Our beliefs about societies include our world views, as well as our assessments about the nature of human nature. Because societies are often densely peopled, we carry images of what we think people are like when we consider the impact of societies on our being and doing—we are points in networks of contacts and communications with others. However, our beliefs about societies influence how we deal with these networks, as well as whether we open our networks, or extend them, to include people we do not know.

Social intelligence requires us to put our beliefs about societies in historical perspectives, so that we understand societies not only in the here and now, but also with respect to trends in their development. There is some evidence, for example, that social justice has progressed in the last few hundred years, through expanding human rights legislation in different societies and internationally. Historical views of societies suggest directions we have already moved in, as well as new directions for future trends and developments. Consequently, our beliefs about societies need to be linked to the passage of time, so that they can serve as effective motivators and orientations for increasing the common good.

It is necessary to continue to learn about societies and modify our beliefs about societies if we are to be socially intelligent, and we benefit from seeking out individuals and groups who can assist us in this endeavor. For example, we learn about societal aspects of our social intelligence more effectively when we find people to teach us, from their knowledge and experiences, how to interpret and understand complex modern and traditional societies. Paying attention to newspaper reports, or media coverage of current affairs, also helps us to meet these challenges, and we frequently learn about current societal influences more effectively when we engage with the work of familiar reporters or journalists. These ways of staying people-oriented, in our search for significant social facts to explain our situations, usually allows us to benefit from more in-depth learning.

Our beliefs about societies must ultimately be our own. In order to accomplish this, we need to spend considerable time examining our knowledge about our own societies and others' societies, as well as scrutinizing our world views. How much do we travel? Where do we travel? Do we explore other societies in our travels, or deepen our bonds with people we already know? Can we use relatives' oral histories of our families to guide us in local or global travel? How can our kin members enlighten us about societies in different times?

In order to become more socially intelligent, we use as many social resources as possible. We try to be creative about our fact-gathering, because it is more important to compare and contrast several people's perspectives on societies, than to understand societies only through impersonal sources of information.

Reviewing our beliefs about societies allows us to assess which beliefs we will keep, refine, or discard. This selection process is easier when we understand not only the social sources of our beliefs, but also the personal underpinnings of our knowledge about societies. Who told us what? Which of our teachers had the most lasting impacts on us? What were their messages about the nature of human nature, and what the world is like? Who defined what our responsibilities are to people in need, or to those we do not know?

Finding sufficient meaningful sources of information about society is an ongoing project. People's views about societies are catalysts which heighten our awareness, and enhance our motivations to increase social justice. Although this agenda cannot always be met, especially when family needs or job demands are pressing, we are more certain that we move toward social justice when we increase our objectivity about self, societies, and world views.

Social Justice

Social intelligence guides us, in our difficult tasks of becoming more objective, by helping us to make critical assessments of our beliefs, and new combinations of beliefs. We become who we want to be by continuing to orient our actions with principles of social intelligence. When we choose our ideals, values, and strategies more deliberately, as well as our beliefs, we see the pragmatic advantages of working toward increasing social justice and the common good.

Just as people are central in our tasks of assessing our beliefs about families, religions, social classes, cultures, and societies, they are also powerful influences on the extent to which we make commitments to social justice. Having social justice orientations and motivations for our actions is not so much a matter of "doing good," as it is a way to solve problems—for example, by settling some of the world's recurring disputes—so that we benefit from a more meaningful

186

life, and a more peaceful coexistence. If we do nothing to resolve conflicts about social injustices, we will gradually lose the glorious diversity of the world we know.

Such goals may have been addressed by our parents, families, religious leaders, teachers, or friends, as well as by public figures at different times of our lives. Nevertheless, unless the ideals of social justice come alive through our own pain, experiences, or observations, they may have little impact on how we conduct our everyday activities. We need to see the depth and limiting effects of social injustices, for example, before we can find the energy and political will to turn our individual and social lives around, in order to better serve social justice.

Becoming socially intelligent allows us to see the extent to which we create our own social problems. Although we are all born into a world of prejudice and discrimination, these conditions are not innate or genetic. Therefore, we can change our social environments and emotional climates, so that our ways of doing things engender cooperation and support, rather than competition, hatred, and injustices. This new way of living is not based on a particular set of beliefs, but rather on considerable awe and reverence for the power of beliefs in our lives, and for our capacities to learn and accomplish changes. The fact that we have not yet been able to design or invent communities and societies, which live according to principles of social intelligence and social justice, does not mean that this is impossible. Our ideals and hopes drive us forward, so that we become more highly motivated to create a better tomorrow.

Enthusiasm is catching, and in order to become sufficiently motivated to accomplish changes which increase social justice, it is useful to find and work together with those who are headed in the same directions. We accomplish more by working cooperatively on social justice issues, for example, than by working alone. Cooperation, not competition, will save us, as well as give more people more access to the common good.

Sharing ideals and visions of possibilities increases our impetus to succeed in difficult, sometimes unrewarding tasks, so that we can persist in our efforts to establish social justice through time.

Enthusiasm is most often generated by sharing ideals and goals, even though disagreements over which means to use to achieve our shared ideals and goals will necessarily persist. We need to work with people who think broadly, and who support principles of social intelligence and social justice, in order to be effective. Even though such people may not come to us, or may not be easily identified—partly because they have not seriously considered issues like social intelligence and social justice— they are nevertheless recognizable by other ideals in their beliefs, intentions, and deeds. We therefore find many different ways to follow, lead, or collaborate with those who are working toward similar ideals and goals.

In order to know what it is in particular that we can accomplish in our moves toward social justice, we should first examine what it is we heard or saw—in relation to significant others of our pasts—that helped us to form our beliefs about social justice. Because these beliefs may have to be modified, knowing their social sources makes our tasks of making such changes more possible. Once we know where we acquired our beliefs in social justice, we become more objective about them, as well as more inclined to change them to make them our own.

When we are adults, the varied influences on our beliefs in social justice tend to be more impersonal. We might have read books, or heard others' views on these topics, for example. However, in order to critically assess our beliefs about social justice, we should scrutinize those authors or impersonal sources that influenced us, so we can be sure we are oriented and motivated by beliefs that mean the most to us.

Although we may not necessarily consider ourselves to be historical actors, when we clarify our beliefs about social justice, or act in concert with others toward increasing social justice, historical awareness should inform the tasks we want to accomplish, as well as principles of social intelligence. Our personal, local, and global awareness empowers our effectiveness as actors, and we respond to historical currents most effectively when we cooperate with those who are also working for social justice.

XI. Ideas and Beliefs

Ideas fuel our beliefs. Whereas we need to be ever vigilant about assessing the meaning and usefulness of our beliefs, we also need to be careful to have as constant and as diverse a flow of ideas feeding into our beliefs as possible. Social intelligence gives us the skills and freedom to look for inspiration and new designs in all sorts of places, and through all kinds of people, so that we can truly use the light of the world to inspire our beliefs and actions.

Ideas frequent our families, religions, social classes, cultures, and societies constantly, and our more familiar ideas often emerge as repeated patterns within, or even among, these significant social spheres. Because what we take for granted—our underlying assumptions about our social situations and our social capacities—is usually made up of familiar patterns of ideas, we should deliberately introduce new ideas into our interactions and exchanges. Our task, then, is to find reliable sources of new ideas that will make a difference to our social intelligence and our goals of social justice. What new ideas about families, religions, social classes, cultures, and societies do we find through our exchanges with friends, in daily news, or by interacting with others in varied social settings? Do these new ideas make sense in light of our goals to work toward increasing social intelligence and social justice? How do people respond to our new or different ideas?

Deliberately dousing our beliefs with fresh ideas renews the vigor and effects of our choices of beliefs. For example, we refine our awareness about important aspects of our societies, when we learn about other countries or other social classes. Also, we assess both social privileges and social disadvantages more accurately when we know about broad ranges of social conditions. Consequently, we see social injustices more easily, and at deeper levels, when we deliberately increase the complexity of our knowledge and ideas about social conditions.

We inevitably open ourselves up to new ideas when we decide to learn as much as we can about a particular social issue, such as gender differences. Learning changes our capacities to understand, and creates new ways of being in our minds, souls, and actions. Considering ideas which explain the impacts of families, religions, social classes, cultures, and societies on gender differences, for example, gives us important new views. These ideas may ultimately inspire us to design innovative strategies to identify or resolve social issues around gender differences, and to increase peaceful coexistence.

The effects of ideas on our beliefs help us to select and modify our old and new beliefs. Social intelligence requires long exploratory phases in this process, whereby we entertain many new ideas and possibilities for individuals, groups, and societies. Some new ideas are immediately more appealing than others, but in the long run, those ideas that affect our beliefs the most, are usually what we find to be the most meaningful and most worthwhile ideas.

Ideas create beliefs, and beliefs give rise to ideas. When we reflect purposefully about our ideas, we make more enlightened choices about which ideas we want to incorporate into our beliefs. When we reflect about our beliefs, we find ideas which prompt us to take new directions in doing what we want to accomplish. Understanding the social origins of our ideas, as well as our beliefs, helps us to appreciate the social contexts and social complexities of our actions more fully, as well as connects us to others in different ways. For example, we do not labor alone when we consider the social conditions of our ideas and beliefs, as well as the social conditions of our particular situations.

Social intelligence helps us to be more selective in pursuing the ideas and beliefs we want to nurture. When we are young, or when we do not have an agenda to increase our social intelligence, we let ideas come and go in our awareness, without paying much attention to them. As we become acquainted with the principles of social intelligence, we consider old and new ideas more carefully, as well as keep our minds open so that we can entertain fresh possibilities for innovations in social conditions. We may discover new ways to learn, for example, which consolidate our knowledge about social classes, or we may link new technologies to more established ways of studying social justice.

All in all, if we want to keep our beliefs about families, religions, social classes, cultures, societies, and social justice current, we should carve out strategies to remain open to new ideas, and to deliberately seek out new ideas. These intellectual habits make us more watchful for new ideas at all times, in spite of our inclinations to be distracted, so that we can create constructive innovations. Honoring the importance of new ideas helps us to design new ways to increase and express our social intelligence, as well as to accomplish social justice.

Families

Our first sources of ideas were our families. As we become adults, we more easily identify the most significant ideas we were exposed to in our families, as well as those relatives who communicated the most ideas to us. Families which are ever open to new ideas generate imaginative and creative family emotional systems, whereas families which habitually resist new ideas develop narrow, pedantic, or stagnant emotional and cultural climates.

As we become more able to assess our families' ideas and the intellectual environments of their ideas—in both the past and the present—we clarify our own views of whether we want to perpetuate how ideas were presented to us by our parents and relatives, or whether we want to create more open, innovative interpretations of our experiences. We may choose to move toward increasing sources of new and fresh ideas from outside our families, for example, because social intelligence shows us that this focus opens windows and doors for members of the next generations of our families. For example, adding new ideas to family exchanges eventually changes patterns in family interactions and relatives' awareness of outside worlds.

When we are too dramatically inventive in introducing new ideas to our families, however, we are usually resisted. Family members predictably object to extreme or frequent innovations, and may present a united front of disapproval to counteract our new-fangled approaches to ideas and decision-making. This does not mean that we should necessarily back down from suggesting new postures to understanding the world, because we know that we are empowered by these social intelligence principles. Furthermore, in the long run, submerging our families in contrasting ideas inevitably serves all family members well, because new life is breathed into our families' beliefs and relatives' established ways of doing things through the new ideas.

New ideas are often associated with young people, and although this may be accurate in some respects, it is usually our most thoughtful family members who present ideas which allow us to see the world differently, or to design new strategies to accomplish ongoing family tasks. It is especially those ideas that shed light on what we want to achieve that should be used to create stronger, more resilient family cultures.

The wisdom of family elders is beneficially incorporated into our searches for new ideas. Even though some of our older family members' ideas may reflect traditions, or past historic times, these ideas can be applied afresh in our modern age of technological discoveries. We may find, for example, that our elders' ideas about crafts or skills help us to deal with current social issues, or specific social problems, so that we meaningfully re-apply ideas that served our elders and ancestors well in the past.

Being in meaningful contact with older relatives gives us a broad array of vivid and tangible contacts with times gone by, which enables us to see the present through ideas from the past. Also, when we collect information about our grandparents or great grandparents, for example, we can usually identify with their past living conditions to some extent—even though they may contrast starkly with our own—as we try to understand these relatives better. Thus, past ideas and experiences may be effective guides for today, in spite of the contrasts in their social situations. The advantages we gain, from using ideas that have weathered time successfully, are that they are seasoned forms of wisdom. For example, older relatives have ideas that still ring true in varied social settings, so that we benefit not only from ideas that may be new to us, but also from ideas that work well in many situations.

Compiling family histories yields additional new ideas about the nature of human nature. What our relatives did in their lifetimes, as well as how they lived, often gives us radical contrasts with present day living conditions and lifestyles. When we imagine the lives of our ancestors, for example, we gain new ideas about how to approach our current everyday lives. Even mundane differences, such as our ancestors' views of time and place, help us to see and live more fully. For example, we can more easily modify our most practical means for adapting to the rapidity and complexity of current social changes, as well as our beliefs about possibilities for social changes, by examining the ideas and social conditions of our ancestors.

Ideas carry us forward, and are incorporated into our beliefs and commitments. Ideas may also disappear quickly if they do not seem to apply directly to our lives. Our task is to avail ourselves of the abundance of ideas in our families. Then we gradually sift through our families' ideas, and select those ideas we think we need. Focusing on what we believe to be the most useful ideas helps us to be discriminating in our selections. Consequently, recognizing which values and facts relate to our ideas and beliefs helps us to be more socially intelligent.

Religions

Religions also embody unique ideas. Religious ideas address sacred or universal dimensions of time and place, and at the same time appeal to our higher, moral selves. Because many religious ideas are integral parts of specific religious beliefs, these ideas may be more compelling than secular ideas. In and of themselves religious ideas sometimes spark revolutions; serve as conservative forces to maintain the status quo; or achieve peace in conflicts.

Religious ideas may inspire us to use social intelligence to increase social justice, or to resolve individual and social problems. Because of their breadth, religious ideas explain universal aspects of our human condition, and suggest ways to develop worldwide religions or religious movements. Furthermore, due to the fact that religious ideas are well-supported by their own religious belief systems, they are mainstays of rituals and commitments which give us religious identities, and make us members of religious communities.

Religious ideas are central in particular religions, and may be common denominators among varied religions. Those religious ideas we choose to make sacred in our beliefs are guiding lights in what we do, and what we want to accomplish. For example, being spiritual may result from applying both religious ideas and principles of social intelligence to our everyday situations or other secular challenges.

When we appeal to religious powers, and use religious ideas to inform our chosen priorities, we often make more progress than if we had not turned to religious ideas for guidance.

Similarly, because religious ideas point us toward spirituality, we may become more rigorous, more highly motivated, or more successful in achieving our collective goals. When we aim to do God's will, for example—a mandate that cuts across several major religions—we are frequently more able to persist in our efforts to do what we think we should be doing, than if we did not particularly want to do God's will.

Religious ideas may calm us when we are troubled, and may inspire prayers or meditations. Religious ideas may also support us, by staying at the back of our active minds while we go about our daily business, and by helping us to meet our most banal responsibilities. Religious ideas are particularly powerful, because they have been used for millennia or centuries before we were born, and because they were often significant, integral parts of our ancestors' lives. We get connected to this grand scope of things by deliberately turning to religions or wisdom literatures as sources for our ideas.

Sometimes religious ideas are so powerful—such as the idea of God's love—that we can meditate on them and use them as guides for a lifetime. In some respects, social justice can be thought of as an aspect of God's love, even though social justice has many secular connotations. The special qualities of religious ideas help us to transcend difficult individual and social conditions, so that we stay focused on our goals, in spite of innumerable hurdles or setbacks. Because religious ideas have proved their powers of endurance, as well as their capacities to support the masses, these are important social resources that we cannot afford to ignore or diminish.

If we set out to increase our social intelligence in a spirit of inquiry, or as a journey, we are free to explore a wide range of religious ideas, not only from the point of view of our own religions, or familiar religions, but also through more exotic religions that we do not know. When we delve more deeply into the ideas of a familiar religion, for example, as well as discover interesting and powerful ideas in new religions, we have more options in selecting religious ideas to refresh our beliefs. Both familiar and new religious ideas guide us to decide which religious ideas we should cultivate as our own, through testing them in our everyday lives.

The means available to us to seek out religious ideas vary, depending on our access to religions and religious ideas. For example, studying religions, speaking with religious believers, hearing sermons or public addresses by religious leaders, taking classes in religions, making commitments to attend religious services, and learning new rituals or new ways to pray and meditate are all sources of religious ideas that flood us with wide ranges of religious ideas, as well as new ways to see ourselves, others, societies, and the world.

Religious ideas strengthen our beliefs, rejuvenate them, or inspire us to formulate new, more meaningful beliefs. We cannot lose anything—and may gain a great deal—by turning to religious ideas to renew our beliefs, motivations, or orientations for actions in the twenty-first century. Even though we may initially have personal or social conflicts about this process, we will ultimately take directions that enlighten our decisions and actions.

Social Classes

At the same time that we develop our social intelligence, we become increasingly aware that we belong to several social classes, depending on our material assets, genders, sexual orientations, races, ethnicities, health, occupations, education, or religions. Because particular ideas are associated with each social class, our ideas inevitably reinforce, contradict, or challenge our beliefs in social classes, ourselves, societies, or globalization.

Ideas are the stuff of education. For example, we expand the number of ideas we have about social classes by learning about different social classes. Who belongs to which social classes? What ideas characterize each social class? Do we stay in our social classes for a lifetime? How do we get out of the social classes we were born into? To what extent do our social classes depend on our beliefs in social classes? Does history change social classes? What or who changes our social classes? How do our social classes restrict us?

Although our beliefs do not determine our social class memberships, they predispose us to identify with particular social classes. We think we belong to a certain social class when we believe we share affinities with members of that social class. For example, even though there are usually no specific foundations of strong identity, or specific shared beliefs underlying our social class memberships, we often feel a sense of community with those who have similar resources, genders, or races. These similarities are reinforced by ideas that characterize our social classes and their lifestyles.

New ideas about social classes challenge or weaken our beliefs about social classes. For example, when we immerse ourselves in a wide range of ideas which challenge our usual social class beliefs, we reduce the push and pull of these beliefs. Educating ourselves about social classes in different societies may break some of our associations between our beliefs about social classes and our social class memberships. Consequently, when our minds are free enough to absorb and use new ideas about social classes or alternatives to social classes, our social class bonds are loosened and become more flexible.

Ideas help us break out of our daily routines. We are refreshed by new ideas because they help us to reassess, more objectively, who we are and how free we are. Because our social classes usually restrict rather than liberate our thoughts, ideals, and actions, we benefit from finding and using new ideas to open up alternative ways of being and doing. Reading new authors, scanning newspapers, going to movies, or talking with friends are relatively easy and accessible activities to undertake, which may at least temporarily detach us from some of our social class situations and limitations.

We also free ourselves from our social class habits by learning new languages or traveling to foreign countries. Undertaking these absorbing activities helps us to see the insularity of our current everyday worlds, so that we get outside our social class perspectives for a while. When we focus on other people's lives, we deepen our understanding of our own, and free ourselves from the most limiting aspects of our social classes.

Studying the history of social classes gives us new ideas about the impermanence of social classes. Peoples' opportunities increase when social justice flourishes, for example, so that social castes become more open social classes. Because we are all caught up in major rhythms of social changes, our social classes as we know them may be temporary in the long run, especially if we have access to education and other sources of ideas that encourage social mobility, or the restructuring of our social classes.

Some ideas have lives of their own that affect social class structures directly. For example, ideas like democracy, equality, or the rule of law can break through the confines of traditional social classes, however compelling these customary social classes are. Also, we are all individual or collective agents, rather than members of social classes. Even though we share many ideas with those who are in the same social classes, we cannot afford to be restricted to these ideas. New ideas are consistently powerful and essential for our progress as individuals, social classes, social movements, and societies.

Because social classes influence our life styles and views of the world at all times, we need to think independently. Our ideas make us independent and different from others, as well as distinctive within our social classes. Furthermore, contrasts in our ideas are frequently catalysts for changing our states of being and doing. Our ideas are crucial in developing our unique potentials, regardless of our social class origins.

Deliberately seeking and focusing on powerful ideas, such as social justice, minimizes our social class influences.

Furthermore, social programs that open up opportunities for less privileged children and adults, for example, are innovations that derive from our ideas, which at the same time break through social class restrictions and traditions. New ideas enlighten our present and future possibilities, so that we increase democracy, improve the quality of life for more people, and foster social justice. Social changes and innovations are sparked by ideas which challenge our social class beliefs, as well as our habitual social class modes of being and doing.

Ideas inspire and recharge our beliefs. They increase our motivations to change social class restrictions. Ideas appeal to us, catch us, and move us along. They derive from social origins, and have the power to transform the status quo throughout our societies. When we deliberately welcome new ideas, we reduce the determining power of our original social class beliefs and social classes.

Cultures

One of the most exciting and invigorating sources of our ideas about self, society, and the world is our cultures. Ideas in our cultures teem and flow without ceasing, and even though they are strongly influenced by past traditions, they are also the essence of freshness, innovation, and change. We know that we are at the cutting edge of great social movements of adaptation or pioneering enlightenment, for example, when we tune into our cultures' ideas—the pulses and heartbeats of our ever-changing cultures.

Ideas from our cultures enliven and renew our beliefs. When our beliefs seem stale, limited, or ineffective we can turn to cultural ideas to challenge them, unsettle them, or reinforce them. Our cultural ideas are the lifeblood of our intentions, motivations, and actions, in that they add new or deeper meanings to how we think and what we do.

Our cultures contain contrasting ideals, expectations, knowledge, religions, education, laws, politics, customs, and traditions as well as more random ideas. We take ideas from these cultural sources to design new artistic images, or to understand whatever goes on around us and within us, including our dreams. We can be destroyed by our cultural ideas, or we can choose ideas that are so creative and so constructive that they direct societies for generations or centuries. Social intelligence places us in a thrilling moment of the present, where and when we become more conscious agents within this tremendous flow of life and enlightened changes. We are integral parts of evolutionary, historical, and ongoing social processes, which enjoin us as global communities and societies.

Increasing our social intelligence requires objectivity and access to facts about our cultures. We enrich our appreciation and understanding of complexities in ourselves, others, and our societies by seeing cultural ideas within and about us. Being more calm and objective helps us to recognize that the pain and suffering of others, as well as our own, are integral parts of the daily social and cultural conditions of many people in historic and contemporary societies. When specific ideas from our cultures enable us to clear our thinking, we are better positioned to design solutions to social problems by increasing social justice.

The culture shock we experience when we travel to unfamiliar places is one of the clearest examples of how new ideas challenge what we take for granted about our own cultures—our languages, customs, habits, and routine transactions with others. When we cross the globe to another hemisphere, or immerse ourselves in cultures which are radically different from our own, alternative worlds open up, so that we see who we are and what we want to accomplish more clearly. This happens because we are cultural beings who need ideas, beliefs, and values in order to exist and survive. Our reasons for staying alive derive from our cultures, and we use cultural ideas to adapt to ongoing social changes.

As human beings we have large, rapidly evolving brains, which may be both our salvation and our downfall. Humans have surmounted numerous obstacles to their survival because they have considered their social conditions, as well as physical solutions to particular survival issues. Even though it is trite to state that we exist because we think, social intelligence reminds us that we think because our cultures are accessible to us throughout our lives. For example, we can only think by using the symbols that our cultures provide so abundantly, and our beliefs need to be clarified, nurtured, and sustained by cultural ideas.

History heightens our awareness that cultures have positive or negative effects on our thriving and surviving. Sometimes our individual choices of beliefs and values run counter to dominant cultural patterns, so these choices may or may not be able to help us to survive as individuals or societies. However, when our cultures do not enhance life, but rather boost destructive forces, our individual preferences are gradually overwhelmed and defeated, which ultimately leads to the destruction of these societies.

By contrast, some cultures lift the conscience and consciousness of their societies, so that these societies prosper and enlighten their populations. Such constructive cultural forces are nurtured and generated by outstanding leaders or social movements, who use cultural ideas to achieve life-enhancing goals. For example, when leaders or social movements successfully introduce new or emergent values to receptive others, the tides of a culture can change a society's direction. In the course of time these constructive, innovative ideas get stronger, and the whole society benefits.

Cultural ideas are contagious. They are historical products that are expressed through a variety of means, so that people carry their best intentions forward to the next generations. Social intelligence increases our awareness of cultural ideas, so that we become players in bringing new beliefs and values, whose time has come, into being. These new beliefs and values improve the quality of life throughout our societies.

In order to set these constructive social and cultural processes in motion, we have to be alert to our own beliefs, as well as to the cultural ideas that feed and nurture our beliefs. Social intelligence guides us in how to make sense of the power and complexity of social and cultural influences in relation to our beliefs, as well as in how to select ideas that save, serve, or prosper new generations as well as ourselves. Our historical fates are in our own hands, and cultural ideas protect us from ourselves and others, especially when we unite with shared purposes like increasing social justice.

Societies

Our societies educate us daily through the complex transactions we enter into each day. If we do not choose to recognize or seek out diversity through our contacts, diversity may overwhelm us. We have to be ready to accept the wide variety of social circumstances that affect us, as well as to be sufficiently versatile in our responses to these conditions, if we are to survive and prosper.

In many respects our dealings with societies entail communicating ideas. Whatever our ideas and beliefs are, we are also barraged by others' ideas and beliefs. Consequently, we have to know what we are about, and how to stand firm in our beliefs, if we are to progress toward our goals. However, it is vital to stay open to others' ideas, because this facilitates our communications, and we continue to be more responsive to others' needs as well as our own.

Respecting ideas that derive from varied societies educates us about the complexities of our shared social circumstances. Even though we may interact only with people in our own societies, the diversity of opinions and experiences in our societies is often tremendous, and we are inevitably affected by wide ranges of ideas. Remaining open to others' ideas helps us to adapt to changing social realities, and to act in new directions.

XI. Ideas and Beliefs

As well as dealing with individuals and groups who are members of different races, classes, and genders in our societies, we must exchange ideas with people from different countries and contrasting cultures. To the extent that our societies have populations that include people from varied backgrounds, we encounter ideas that derive from contrasting situations. Furthermore, high rates of immigration enliven and fertilize exchanges of ideas among people from different countries, even though there may be conflicts of interest and altercations in some international exchanges.

One of the common characteristics of transactions with people from different backgrounds, within our own societies, is that they are largely impersonal. Because we meet many anonymous strangers in the course of a day, we need to develop codes of courtesies, as well as ways to listen and learn from others, if we are to be effective in our communications and well-intentioned endeavors. Strangers are aware of our different degrees of acceptance of their ideas, for example, so that even though we may not consistently agree with them, we need to demonstrate some understanding and appreciation of their ideas. Participating in reciprocal communications is invaluable, because we both listen to others, and depend on them to be there to listen to our ideas.

Reading newspapers, studying historical and current research or commentaries on societies, and continuing interpersonal exchanges with people from different societies deepen the meaningfulness of our give and take in ideas. New ideas enliven our beliefs, and make our daily actions and adaptations more effective, because when we understand how societies work—through social intelligence—we become more successful in achieving our goals.

Ideas about our societies flow from our personal contacts, as well as from political and social leaders. Whenever possible, we need to put our ideas about our societies in broad international contexts, so that we can assess how other societies' ideas affect our day-to-day conduct. Race, class, and gender are international as well as national social influences, for example, which generate their own flows of ideas.

Because ideas from our societies, and from international communities, are fluid, they become vital raw materials for creativity and inspiration. Ideas are the lifeblood of what we think, say, and do, and can be used for a wide variety of purposes. Social intelligence shows us some of the most constructive ways to employ our ideas, so that they become embodied in our beliefs, and create constructive social changes.

Social intelligence also helps us to consider our societies as whole systems, which have varied ideas and impacts on our behavior. We assess our societal ideas by considering what it means to be an American, an American woman, or an American man. Which ideas are associated with being an historical actor in the present? Which ideas most usefully guide us in our work in society?

As children, we were forced to participate in formal learning projects, whether we wanted to or not. As adults, we see more clearly that because we must understand important ideas in our societies, we need to study their social origins and social consequences, taking sufficient time to grasp important but unfamiliar ideas. A variety of rich sources of ideas sheds light on, and gives depth to, our ideas about societies. For example, browsing in local public libraries shows us how local and regional ideas are expressed through historical documents and narratives. Whatever means we choose to access information about our societies' past and present, ideas provide us with new meanings that refresh and energize our beliefs. Thus ideas about our societies prevent our beliefs about societies from becoming too rigid, and they point us in new directions.

Teaching others about societies' ideas clarifies our understanding of these ideas. If we make commitments to teach, we usually assume responsibilities for communicating knowledge about our societies and the world to members of younger generations. This practice puts us in touch with the future, because young people pass on our societies' and the world's ways of doing things, in order to deal with infinite unknown circumstances.

Communicating or teaching societies' ideas through time helps us to understand history, and changes meanings associated with particular societies. Increasing diversity—especially through shifts in social classes, races, and genders—compels us to use new perspectives to formulate ideas and beliefs. Our changed world views precipitate new behavior patterns, and we are carried forward by our more refined and more powerful ideas and beliefs. Thus, being socially intelligent prevents us from stagnating, and enables us to meet successfully the necessary transitions involved in building new societies.

Social Justice

Social justice is both an idea and a complex cluster of ideas. In spite of the wide range of interpretations of the idea of social justice, there are some common denominators of meanings. For example, social intelligence claims that individual, group, and societal progress depend on moving toward achieving social justice, rather than on actually achieving social justice. Therefore, in important respects, social justice is a series of social processes and negotiations which eventually culminate in accomplishing considerable degrees of equality, inclusiveness, diversity, cooperation, and openness.

Social justice has direct meanings for most adults, as well as implied meanings. The idea of social justice has played different roles in societies' histories. It is a major cultural theme that is sometimes apparent, or ignored, by populations for long or short periods of time. Because social justice usually has only sporadic influences in populations and societies, awareness about needs to increase the common good—and its accessibility—for all members of populations may not resonate in some societies.

In spite of a history of infrequent successes, the idea of social justice can galvanize large groups of people, especially the less privileged or dispossessed. When people become aware that they lack privileges, for example, they frequently turn to the idea and ideal of social justice, so that they can become better coordinated in their aims, intentions, and goals. When groups are not satisfied with their rewards, or lack rewards, with respect to majorities in their societies, they are more likely to organize around different ideas or principles, such as social justice.

Among all ideas, social justice has considerable power to inspire us, or to guide our searches for more meaningful beliefs, purposes, and objectives. Even though we may believe that social justice is an impossible ideal, rather than a practical idea, we can still turn toward social justice when we want to inspire our thoughts, beliefs, and actions. This begins to transform our lives, intentions, and beliefs. We start to assess our experiences more objectively, for example, by comparing our lives with and without social justice as an idea, goal or inspiration.

Social intelligence starts with ideas other than the idea of social justice. For example, either the idea that we control our destinies more effectively by understanding the power and complexity of major social influences in our lives, or the idea that we increase our effectiveness in society by dealing directly with social influences, helps us to begin to build the knowledge base of social intelligence. Then, a more advanced idea of social intelligence is that when we understand the facts of our social situations, we improve our contributions as historical actors, and increase the common good.

Social intelligence embraces the fact that each individual understands and interprets social justice differently, with the result that individuals' actions toward social justice objectives vary considerably. Social intelligence also suggests that working collectively to achieve social justice consolidates individual interpretations of the idea and ideal of social justice, because collective actions predictably achieve more than individual efforts.

These aspects of cooperation show that social justice is an idea that has powerful organizational and motivational consequences. For example, the idea of social justice moves nations to act when political wills are receptive. Also, the idea of social justice may transform individuals' beliefs and motives, as well as their day-to-day actions. However, the idea of social justice is less effective when it is not founded on, or supported by, social intelligence. For example, we need to know how social influences govern the outcomes of our behavior before we can make our most effective commitments to social justice. If we increase our social intelligence first, and then turn to the ideas and practices of social justice for inspiration and motivation, we are more adept at coordinating our individual and collective efforts to expand the common good.

After laboring arduously to develop our social intelligence, we can immediately refresh our beliefs and views of the facts of our situations by considering the idea of social justice. The powerful idea of social justice provides historical perspectives, as well as new ways to understand how families, beliefs, social classes, cultures, and societies are constantly in play as significant social influences on our individual and collective well-being.

In some circumstances, examining our lives through social justice concerns and issues turns us toward increasing our own and others' social intelligence. We realize that social influences are strong forces to be reckoned with, and that we need to understand their power and complexity more deeply, before we can be successful in our individual and collective social justice endeavors. The idea of social justice helps us to establish our priorities: it turns us toward the idea of social intelligence, as well as toward the idea that we need to work with others to establish social justice. Furthermore, as we make these changes in our priorities, we are more likely to accomplish social justice.

XII. Values and Beliefs

Social intelligence shows us how our values anchor our beliefs. Values are syntheses of individuals' beliefs, and are extended and personalized by our beliefs. When we look toward the kind of world we are creating in the present and future, we need to make sure that we are perpetuating those particular values that we think serve humankind best. For example, we need to ask ourselves questions about the world we want to bring into being for our grandchildren and great grandchildren, and the world we want to set in motion for the rest of the twenty-first century.

Because our values cut across societies, politics, cultures, social classes, races, ethnic groups, genders, religions, and families, we should be as clear as possible about choosing the most constructive values for all concerned. Social intelligence helps us to clarify our value choices as well as our beliefs, and turns us in directions that increase rather than decrease social justice. Increasing our social intelligence is some guarantee that we have done all we can to orient our societies toward better futures rather than worse futures.

Social intelligence shows us that whatever values we honor the most through our beliefs and actions become empowered in our societies. In some respect our values and beliefs are important players in a numbers game: populations' particular values and beliefs, as well as the values and beliefs of the dominant few, compete for social honor and power.

Unfortunately, the dominant few in societies often force their values and beliefs on others, so that their values and beliefs are difficult to avoid or neutralize. Therefore, although we all have value choices, some votes have more influence than others. However, the more we act collectively—with constructive, socially intelligent values and beliefs—the more likely we are to bring these constructive values and beliefs to fruition in societies in the long run.

In order to achieve clarity about which values we want to reinforce, and in order to assess our passive inclinations to stay safe, we must make active commitments to understand and tackle the obstacles or threats that inevitably waylay us, as we increase our social intelligence and work toward social justice. Unless we recognize and deal directly with values, such as consumerism, which have significant negative impacts on our populations, we usually do whatever is easiest, discovering later—to our chagrin—that we inadvertently created a world we do not want to have.

Social traditions are meaningful starting points, rather than end points, in our journeys toward global social justice. Social traditions are established, entrenched ways of doing things, which frequently restrict opportunities for many people— perhaps even for majorities within populations. Because of these social facts about traditions, we should use social intelligence to define new ways of doing things collectively in societies, so that we express ideas and ideals of equality, inclusiveness, diversity, cooperation, and openness in our transactions with others and the world. Such an approach strengthens these constructive values, so that we create the kind of world for which we yearn.

Our shared trajectory in this direction moves us away from the opposite values of inequality, exclusiveness, homogeneity, competitiveness, and closure in communications or transactions. Some of the destructive social conditions of alienation that arise from focusing on these restrictive values are isolation, meaninglessness, powerlessness, and self-estrangement. Social intelligence shows us that unless we make active, collective efforts to reverse such unfavorable social conditions, our worlds of tomorrow will not be what we prefer.

Making constructive changes in our values and beliefs requires that we stand up and say that our current conditions are unacceptable, and that we must actively pursue new directions to strengthen more positive values. It is only when our beliefs and actions focus on constructive values, and become sufficiently widely accepted, that we create more innovative and more beneficial societies for the future.

Using principles of social intelligence helps us to go further in these optimal directions, especially when we are motivated and committed to make whatever changes are necessary to achieve these goals through our day-to-day values and beliefs. For example, utopian realities are more attainable when we use the guidance of social intelligence to inspire our choices in values and beliefs, at the same time that we work toward social justice. When we pursue socially intelligent ideals, we clarify our visions of possibilities as well as keep better futures in mind as we act in the present.

We gain control over our value choices when we know what our beliefs are, and act in accordance with this awareness at all times. Ultimately we must also ask ourselves which particular values we cherish the most, and which values we think we should cherish, in order to build a socially intelligent world that moves toward social justice through truly sharing a greater common good.

Families

Although there is much public discourse, as well as much disagreement, about what "family values" are, social intelligence suggests that it is more important to concentrate on the value we place on our families, than on the specific values of our very different family cultures. In other words, it is more useful and more effective to give primacy to the importance of our families in determining our choices and world views, than it is to define which particular traditional, religious, or philosophical values our families have or should have. Furthermore, when we concentrate on understanding the emotional impact our families have on our values, beliefs, and decisions, we become less vulnerable to being side-tracked by discovering which particular cultural values our families express or should express.

When we examine the impacts of our families on formulating our values, we see that family processes—or patterns of family interactions—largely determine how we perceive ourselves and the world, and how we value ourselves and the world. By contrast, when we focus on relatively impersonal values, such as truth or worldly success, we easily lose sight of the social or family origins of these values. Consequently, we are less able to change these values if necessary. Unless we understand some of the direct links between our values and our family dependencies, we have to use will power—rather than critical understanding—to change our values, which is often ineffective in the long run.

When we research the social or family origins of our values, we see more clearly how we were influenced to accept particular values, and we begin to unravel and redo family impacts on our thinking, being, and acting where necessary. Recognizing power relations in our families is often a key to understanding the pressures that were brought to bear on valuing education, for example, when we were young. When the value we place on education works well for us, there is no real need to change our family interactions around this issue. However, if we want to place a higher priority on education, we need to have different exchanges with our relatives. Becoming more socially intelligent is a reliable start to making lasting changes about valuing education more highly, so that we can pursue particular lines of study or professional development.

XII. Values and Beliefs

Going back to family sources of our values shows us the extent to which we were coerced, when we were young, to accept parents' or grandparents' views of education or other values. Also, we became religious, for example, due more to our parents' pressures and parents' religious practices, than to our own divine enlightenment.

Although we frequently tend to accept our families' educational or religious beliefs and values at deep levels of our being, we may do so primarily because these were important to our parents or siblings when we were young. Discussing education or religion directly with our parents and siblings helps us to loosen the grip that our values and beliefs have on us, so that we can more easily make necessary changes among our values and beliefs.

When we consider values in other spheres of our lives, such as social mobility, we again most usefully start our searches for the social origins of our beliefs through our knowledge of our families' dependencies. Just as families play dominant roles in socializing us into religions, they are equally influential in orienting us to more secular values such as education, social classes, gender, and social justice. Rather than merely help us to avoid family influences in formulating our values, social intelligence deepens our understanding of the power that family influences have on our values and beliefs. This encourages us to free ourselves from family influences which we do not want, while at the same time we continue to examine past and present patterns of family interactions that still create and reinforce our current values and beliefs.

It is particularly important to deal with family connections to our values and beliefs, because this knowledge allows us to be more autonomous in making socially intelligent decisions. When we become more socially intelligent, we have more control over our destinies, and make more substantial contributions to the common good. We achieve objectivity about ourselves best by looking closely at our past and continuing family dependencies, and by changing imbalances we find through examining how we embraced our values and beliefs in the first place.

From an historical perspective, understanding our values and their family origins has the potential to influence how we do things for decades, as well as in the present. We often stay emotionally attached to our values of the past because they feel comfortable, but unless they serve us well, we will not be able to accomplish what we want to do. Increasing our social intelligence gives us reliable ways to assess our values and our beliefs, as well as their impacts on our behavior. Consequently, we can unsnarl and neutralize the power of our most troublesome emotional dependencies on what we do, and on what we want to do.

Religions

Many of our values and beliefs derive from our religions. When we are religious, we essentially commit ourselves to clusters of related values and beliefs. These values and beliefs form a sacred belief system, which often predisposes us to act in particular ways in everyday situations. To some extent we can predict others' values and beliefs when we know what their religions are, in the same way that we can predict their secular values and beliefs when we know what their political parties or occupations are.

This clustering of values and beliefs around religious or secular belief systems is a powerful influence on our choices and behavior. Clusters of values and beliefs persist, largely because it is easier for us to act in relation to clear-cut, established religious belief systems, than to assess our values individually in every changing circumstance. Because we are often indoctrinated with religious values and beliefs at young ages, having religious values and beliefs—whatever they are— are experienced as being "right," "good," or "natural." Unfortunately, when we feel that we do not need to assess our values and beliefs in our everyday situations, we tend to live automatically, without considering the consequences of our actions.

If accepting others' religious values and beliefs as our own works well for us, so be it. Perhaps there is no real need here to scrutinize how we acquired our religions, unless things seem too good to be true, or questionable, for at least some of the time. Social intelligence requires us to acquire and maintain a sufficiently high level of general social awareness, so that we can identify and modify difficulties or challenges that derive from using others' values and beliefs as our own. Social intelligence also shows us that we should avoid becoming complacent, because this enables us to ignore or hide the many subtle ways in which we allow our values and beliefs to cancel each other out, leading to ineffective decisions and actions.

Our religions' values and beliefs provide ways to understand ourselves, human nature, others, societies, and the world. However, they produce powerful assumptions, sometimes implicit rather than explicit, which often limit our abilities to fully understand social influences. Furthermore, when our religions' values and beliefs are supported by sacred sanctions, they affect our behavior even more strongly.

If we value the word of God as our commandment, for example, or believe that God has a will for us to accomplish, our motives and orientations to actions may be narrowed and intensified. Also, we often choose to do God's commandment, or God's will, rather than accomplish secular goals, when we have religious values and beliefs. Thus, because our interpretations of divine intent may permeate all our decisions and actions when we are religious, we must be sure that our underlying religious values and beliefs are truly our own.

One advantage of living according to religious values and beliefs is that religions have proved that they can sustain many individuals—even populations—in varied circumstances. Unlike many secular values and beliefs, the staying power and endurance of religions has been demonstrated throughout history, and individuals can gain many benefits from belonging to religious communities, which may span whole nations or the globe, as well as local regions. Our human frailties have been accepted, supported, directed, and inspired by religious values and beliefs through the ages.

When some traditional religious purposes and supports do not work for us, however, we should look elsewhere for guides about how to act, as well as for missions to fulfill. Social intelligence is a source of strength, not only for those who have religious values and beliefs, but also for those who want to use their secular knowledge and experiences as foundations for building understanding, purpose, and direction in the world. Because we are social beings, we need to heighten our awareness of what is going on in our lives, as well as decide how to live, so that we build a better world today for tomorrow.

Social intelligence helps us to be both critical of and responsible for our assessments of ourselves and our worlds. When we use our social intelligence to understand the power of social influences, we open up additional ways to understand the universe, rather than accept limited knowledge on a "blind faith" basis.

Social intelligence helps us to deliberately choose our values, so that we can regulate our beliefs and their expressions as values more effectively. We can also ask the important question of what particular religious values we need to cherish, in order to build a socially intelligent world. In this way we work toward social justice, and embody values such as equality, inclusiveness, diversity, cooperation, and openness in whatever we do.

Social Classes

Our social classes are characterized by specific values and beliefs, which express the cultures of their social class members. If we are members of a lower class, for example, we

218

have lifestyles and goals that reflect lower class values and beliefs. Or, if we are women, we have lifestyles and goals that reflect women's values and beliefs. Because our social class memberships overlap and cut across each other, they have complex relationships among themselves, which make some of the links between the values and beliefs of different social classes difficult to define or assess.

Social intelligence encourages us to select social classes that are meaningful to us, rather than merely to accept the social class definitions and hierarchies used by most societies. When we are more socially intelligent, we understand how we can honor our individual differences more fully, through cultivating social class affiliations that reflect our own interests and talents.

Choosing, or even inventing, our own social class categories makes us more satisfied and more empowered, for example, than if we automatically repeat others' social class categories and systems. However, we must neutralize the influences of the more conventional social class categories that others use, in order to gain sufficient freedom and autonomy to design innovative and meaningful social class categories for ourselves.

When we select social classes, like race and ethnicity, to define who we are, we need to recognize the complex ways in which values and beliefs reinforce or challenge these class differences. For example, we should examine issues related to race and ethnic social classes, such as whether we value race and ethnicity as desirable characteristics in a richly diverse society. Or assess to what extent we think of social classes based on race and ethnicity as strengthening and sustaining dominant elites. Do we understand how race and ethnic class differences affect health concerns? How do values and beliefs related to sexual orientations affect race and ethnic social classes?

Social intelligence helps us to recognize the impacts of social classes, as well as suggests ways to neutralize the more negative values that social classes have. Social intelligence also shows us that when we think of individuals and groups as having intrinsic qualities, rather than as competitors for fixed resources, we can move beyond the limitations that necessarily accompany hierarchical social classes.

For example, when we do not value social classes as significant, competitive interest groups, we build more tolerance, as well as more understanding within and among our populations, especially when we realize that there are often no real needs to compete for social class statuses. Valuing more egalitarian relationships increases the meaningfulness of our lives, because we stereotype others less, and accept them more fully than is possible in hierarchical social class systems.

Social intelligence helps us to be more objective about our social situations. When we view social classes more objectively, we see the flaws and restrictions of social class hierarchies more clearly, as well as question whether or not we want to participate in societies' social class pressures to compete for upward social mobility. Valuing social classes less makes us freer to choose downward social class mobility, for example, or to position ourselves more securely within our own interest groups. Consequently, we no longer allow ourselves merely to repeat social class traditions to compete for fixed resources in our societies, but rather work toward increasing social justice.

When we choose to nurture values and beliefs which do not directly reflect traditional social class value systems, we gain new kinds of freedom. We are freer agents when we design our own social class memberships, for example, because then we make commitments to groups which represent our real interests. By contrast, when we operate only within established social class systems, we may spend our lives pursuing goals which largely reflect upward social class mobility, without addressing our deepest needs and interests.

From historical viewpoints, and through social intelligence, we see the importance of striving to attain values and beliefs that enlighten us and our societies, rather than values and beliefs which deepen social class rivalries and competitiveness. Social intelligence guides us to realize that we can have improved futures, because many of our values and beliefs inspire quests to create better worlds today for tomorrow.

Thus, there is no real need to establish additional contemporary social class markers, which necessarily organize or restrict opportunities and rewards among members of upper, middle, and lower social classes. Rather, social intelligence inspires us to design new communities and new societies, with increased possibilities for cooperation, so that we can increase social satisfaction and establish social justice.

Cultures

Values and beliefs are the essence of our family, local, national, and global cultures. What we do, as well as how we do things, reflects the meanings we attribute to our actions, which derive from our cultures. Furthermore, the meanings we attach to our actions may be so important that our styles of conducting our daily business become more influential than the specific tasks we accomplish. Ultimately our beliefs reflect cultural values, and our choices in beliefs are value choices. Similarly, our decisions and commitments to work toward increasing social intelligence or social justice, which derive from our deepest parts of self, reflect cultural values.

Our cultures are determined, in part, by the level of economic development of our societies. This is why modern materialistic values are strong components of contemporary industrialized societies. Societies which do not have modern economies are generally ruled more by tradition and custom than by legislation, having more cultural values related to skills and crafts than to advanced technologies. In either case, however, our cultures are consistently powerful influences on how we relate to each other, and on what we value as our ideals, objectives, and goals.

Cultures maintain and support our social classes, as well as how we act as men and women in our societies. Our educational and legal systems express our cultural values directly, as do our knowledge and technologies. Cultures are so pervasive, and so contagious in their impacts, that social intelligence confirms that our societies need cultural foundations in order to thrive and survive. Similarly, our social problems, together with our destructive practices of prejudice and discrimination, are cultural products.

When we consider the conditions necessary to bring about constructive historical or social changes, we see that cultures may herald new pathways to the future by focusing on particular values, like education. By contrast, cultures may also lag behind developments in societies by privileging traditions, or by turning toward religions rather than sciences. Our individual and collective positions on social change inevitably reflect our values. When we are discomforted by modern ways of doing things, for example, we tend to resist change and focus on traditions of the past. Over all, however, we need to choose values and cultures to orient us toward past, present, or future conditions in our societies.

When we consider beliefs and social intelligence, we see that values are often our ultimate sources of inspiration. Whether we value traditional forms of wisdom, or intuitive sparks of enlightenment, our higher selves are inevitably influenced by the cultures of our beliefs. Similarly, our different levels of social intelligence reflect values we have made our own, as well as our awareness of social justice issues and practices. We are who we are because of our value choices, and we will be who we will be because of our value choices.

Recognizing the power of values in our everyday lives connects us to influential social currents in societies. We are not alone when we strive for particular values or ideals, or when we turn toward social justice for inspiration, purpose, and direction. Furthermore, we are also more able to work cooperatively with others, or to achieve collective goals, when we connect our beliefs to social values. Values show us ways to be and act in relation to like-minded others, as well as to societies.

During our life courses, our commitments to particular values often result from our family dependencies. However, we frequently try to change our families' values as we reach adulthood, due to our many years of education and our political participation in local or national groups. Even though we may think that our commitments to values are flexible aspects of our behavior, we will need to deliberately modify our beliefs, so that we can change our past and continuing values more easily.

Changing our beliefs predictably changes our values, or we become more able to coordinate our values. Changing our beliefs may also reduce the number of contradictions among our values and beliefs, so that we can achieve more of our goals and ideals in our everyday lives.

Our values and beliefs are important mechanisms whereby our cultures keep up with historic times, and avoid lagging behind other social changes. Sometimes our cultures are beacons for the future, rather than means to reconstruct or reinstate disappearing traditions. Our individual and collective values and beliefs are integral parts of broad cultural and social changes, which enable us to stay open and committed to social justice, in order to build more rewarding lives for all.

Societies

Societies are usefully thought of as political units—usually nation states—that sometimes change their boundaries and names over time. In spite of current strong globalization trends, and the relatively rapid growth of a single global market economy, many distinctive societies persist with their own cultures and national identities. We often pay allegiance to this societal distinctiveness through our shared feelings of national pride and patriotism.

Social intelligence does not support the cultivation of intense, "blind" patriotism, because this is usually characterized by strong ethnocentrism, as well as marked feelings of moral superiority. Allegiances to extreme nationalism tend to engender hatreds that do not contribute constructively to sharing planet earth with other societies in cooperative, workable ways. By contrast, being socially intelligent requires that we balance our appreciation of national distinctiveness with awareness of being members of the same international community, thereby seeking a common good that addresses both national and international needs for peaceful coexistence.

Just as our cultures are made up of different social values, our societies are also based on social values. Although these values may overlap each other, societies are usually more concerned than cultures about maintaining values that reinforce our national interests and national security, values that maintain our political independence, and values that yield a reliable balance of power among different societies. We are political beings, as well as cultural and social beings, and our choices of political values necessarily reflect our needs to survive as individuals and societies.

Whether we want to or not, our civic responsibilities—to participate in maintaining optimal conditions in our societies—require that we adopt values that contribute directly to societies' well-being. Thus, as well as making choices among social values, we need to identify political designs and interventions that we want to support nationally and internationally. Although we may not be called upon to articulate these choices frequently, we can sometimes choose to support or reject the use of political force in situations that threaten societies' security.

Our societal and political values influence our beliefs, and our beliefs influence our values. Although we move in public social spheres when we enter into discourses about social and political values, our deliberately selected personal beliefs also inform our interests in values. Being an historical actor, for example, focuses our attention on values that either bring about social changes or resist social changes. Being an historical actor may also encourage us to take responsibility for international shifts in the balance of power among different societies.

Although these broad social influences seem remote from our earliest family influences on our beliefs and values, the emotional roots of our initial world views frequently come into play when we examine the scope of our political interests. Understanding how the emotional systems of families interact gives us clues to understand how national and international relations become overburdened by the emotions we invest in specific nationalities, patriotism, or strategies and techniques to bring about social or political changes. When we are socially intelligent, we apply our knowledge of family emotional systems to varied social systems, so that we gain needed clarity in complex and intense social or political situations.

Some of the meanings and purposes that enlighten our choices of political values derive from our new or continuing investments in social justice. Just as we make decisions about local and national actions according to ideals and principles of social justice, we also use social justice to guide our participation in global changes. By choosing to maintain values associated with social justice—such as equality, inclusiveness, diversity, cooperation, and openness—we necessarily act to increase the common good, as well as social intelligence, throughout the world.

Being socially intelligent, and aiming to increase social justice, are foundations for our political identities. Social intelligence and social justice also help us to balance our needs to be patriotic with our needs to be cooperative. For example, we cannot build a satisfactory global society for the future, without paying attention to our specificity as individuals and societies, at the same time that we acknowledge our existential needs to share planet earth with other societies in practical, equitable ways. Our values and beliefs connect us to these vital issues, and we vote yea or nay for the worlds we want through our actions.

Social Justice

When we act according to principles of social intelligence, we move toward achieving social justice. We value social justice because we recognize that it is a way out of the many dilemmas that exist in today's world, and because social justice suggests meaningful and peaceful directions for populations to take. Social justice is a pragmatic strategy to achieve global changes that increase the common good for all. The usefulness of social justice makes it an important goal of being socially intelligent, and explains why it is socially intelligent to pursue social justice.

Social intelligence calls out the strongest and best in us, so that we can cooperate with each other to produce enrichments that benefit all. The fact that we have not yet been able to achieve social justice on a large scale, or for long periods of time, does not mean that social intelligence and social justice are impossible ideals. Rather they are values that are incorporated in particular beliefs, which we can continue to cultivate throughout our lifetimes.

When we are socially intelligent, we apply the values and beliefs of social justice to our families, religions, social classes, cultures, and societies, so that these crucial building blocks of our global community become stronger and wiser. We also use the values and beliefs of social justice as motivations and orientations for our actions, which ultimately improve social conditions in societies. Furthermore, when we are able to formulate realistic, as well as idealistic, plans for our worlds today and tomorrow, we free ourselves from repeating some of our contradictory or unworkable traditions and mistakes of the past.

Perhaps most of all, the values and beliefs of social intelligence and social justice help us to think outside the box of conventional thinking, so that we imagine and work toward constructing communities and societies that have not yet existed. Although our visions of tomorrow must ultimately be clarified through time, so that they can be articulated with some degree of precision, investing in our values and beliefs about social intelligence and social justice in present situations is sufficient to move us in these directions.

Social intelligence is a foundation for applying social justice in problem-solving ventures. We cannot create effective strategies to change destructive patterns in social influences in today's societies, unless we have a sufficiently high level of awareness of how we are restricted by social influences in our day-to-day exchanges. For example, when we free ourselves from overly burdensome family dependencies, damaging religious beliefs, limited social class views, cultural fads, and destructive societal trends, we innovate more successfully. This freedom enables us to design social strategies that create more peaceful and more productive social conditions for our coexistence on planet earth.

However, if we move ahead too quickly—for example, by trying to establish social justice before we have a deep understanding of the nature of human nature—we are likely to fail in our endeavors. We need social intelligence to know what we are about, and we must live our social intelligence sufficiently deeply, in order to succeed in bringing about increased social justice. Social intelligence makes social justice possible through our considered choices in values, beliefs, ideals, and daily practices.

When we become historical actors, we increase our social intelligence by changing our patterns of interaction. As we do this we gain objectivity, and increase our compassion for others. At the same time, we let go of our ethnocentrism, prejudice, and discrimination, so that we can focus more exclusively on what it means to be human, and what it means to share planet earth with others. We become more realistic, because we recognize the power and tenacity of social influences that affect our lives. We also use social intelligence to find social wisdom, so that we can sustain our work in social justice, as well as teach principles of social intelligence and social justice to others.

Applying social intelligence and social justice requires us to take charge of our values and beliefs, in order to live with disagreements as well as agreements. Our values and beliefs about equality, inclusiveness, diversity, cooperation, and openness motivate us to continue to make the world of tomorrow more livable than our current world. Moreover, when we pass on ideas and principles of social intelligence and social justice to members of younger generations, we ensure that this future is more likely to happen.

Suggested Reading

Arana, Marie. 2001. *American Chica: Two Worlds, One Childhood.* NewYork: Random House.

Archley, Robert C. 2000. *Social Forces and Aging, 9th ed.* Belmont, CA: Wadsworth.

Barber, Benjamin R. 1995. *Jihad vs. McWorld: How Globalism and Tribalism are Reshaping the World.* New York: Random House.

Berger, Peter. 1963. *Invitation to Sociology.* New York: Doubleday.

Berger, Peter L., and Thomas Luckmann. 1966. *The Social Construction of Reality.* Garden City, NY: Doubleday.

Bowen, Murray. 1978. *Family Therapy in Clinical Practice.* New York: Jason Aronson.

Calasanti, Toni M., and Kathleen F. Slevin. 2001. *Gender, Social Inequalities and Aging.* Walnut Creek, CA: AltaMira Press.

Collins-Lowry, Sharon M. 1996. *Black Corporate Executives.* Philadelphia, PA: Temple University Press.

Du Bois, W. E. B. 1994/1903. *The Souls of Black Folk.* New York: Dover Publications.

Freedman, Estelle B., and John D'Emilio. 1988. *Intimate Matters: A History of Sexuality in America.* New York: Harper and Row.

Gallagher, Sally K. 2003. *Evangelical Identity and Gendered Family Life.* New Brunswick, NJ: Rutgers University Press.

Gans, Herbert J. 1999. *Popular Culture and High Culture: An Analysis and Evaluation of Taste.* New York: Basic Books.

Gardner, Howard. 1983. *Multiple Intelligences.* New York: Basic Books.

Gerstl, Naomi, Dan Clawson, and Robert Zussman, eds. 2002. *Families at Work: Expanding the Boundaries.* Nashville, TN: Vanderbilt University Press.

Giddens, Anthony. 1999. *Runaway World: How Globalization is Shaping Our Lives.* London: Profile Books.

Gitlin, Todd. 2002. *Media Unlimited: How the Torrent of Images and Sounds Overwhelms Our Lives.* New York: Metropolitan Books.

Goffman, Erving. 1959. *The Presentation of Self in Everyday Life.* Garden City, NY: Doubleday.

Goffman, Erving. 1963. *Stigma: Notes on the Management of Spoiled Identity.* Englewood Cliffs, NJ: Prentice Hall.

Kanter, Rosabeth Moss. 1977. *Men and Women of the Corporation.* New York: Basic Books.

Kerr, Michael E., and Murray Bowen. 1988. *Family Evaluation.* New York: W. W. Norton.

Suggested Reading

Mills, C. Wright. 1959. *The Sociological Imagination.* New York: Oxford University Press.

Schwartz, Pepper, and Virginia Rutter. 1998. *The Gender of Sexuality.* Thousand Oaks, CA: Pine Forge Press.

Starr, Paul. 1982. *The Social Transformation of American Medicine.* New York: Basic Books.

Wilson, Bryan. 1982. *Religion in Sociological Perspective.* New York: Oxford University Press.

Wuthnow, Robert. 1998. *After Heaven: Spirituality in America Since the 1950s.* Berkeley, CA: University of California Press

With many thanks to my colleagues at Georgetown University Sociology and Anthropology Department, the Bowen Center for the Study of the Family, Association for Applied and Clinical Sociology, and the Commission on Applied and Clinical Sociology. I am also indebted to my clients and students, who have taught me so much, and of course to my wonderful American and English families, who continue to put up with me on a daily basis.

www.ingramcontent.com/pod-product-compliance
Lightning Source LLC
Chambersburg PA
CBHW030427290526
45786CB00001B/177